To Martin.

from Barbara.

Christmas 1977

SOCIAL HISTORY
OF EDWARDIAN BRITAIN

Other titles in the same series:
The Illustrated London News
Social History of Victorian Britain
by Christopher Hibbert

SOCIAL HISTORY
OF EDWARDIAN BRITAIN

BY JAMES BISHOP

ANGUS & ROBERTSON · PUBLISHERS

ANGUS & ROBERTSON · PUBLISHERS
London · Sydney · Melbourne · Singapore · Manila

First published by Angus and Robertson (UK) Ltd
2 Fisher Street, London, WC1, in 1977

Foreword Copyright © Sir Charles Petrie
Text Copyright © James Bishop 1977
Illustrations © *The Illustrated London News* 1977
ISBN 0 207 95762 2
Series devised by Anthony Gould
Designed by Adrianne LeMan
Picture research and index by Elisabeth Emberson
Printed and bound in Great Britain by
Morrison & Gibb Ltd, London and Edinburgh

CONTENTS

ACKNOWLEDGEMENTS

Most of the illustrations in this book have been reproduced from contemporary issues of *The Illustrated London News*. The remainder have been taken from *The Sketch, The Graphic, The Sphere,* and *The Illustrated Sporting and Dramatic News,* sister papers which began publication some time after *The Illustrated London News*, and which have since ceased publication and now form part of the archives and Picture Library of *The Illustrated London News*.

Quotations in the text have been taken from a number of published works, and the author acknowledges his debt to many of the books listed in the Bibliography, and in particular to Sir Philip Magnus, whose biography *King Edward VII* (John Murray 1964), remains the standard work from which all studies of the period must now begin. For permission to quote from the following works acknowledgement is made to J. B. Priestley, for the quotation from *The Edwardians* (Heinemann, 1970); to Sir Charles Petrie, for quotations from *Scenes from Edwardian Life* (Eyre & Spottiswoode, 1965); to Hutchinson & Co Ltd, for the quotation from W. MacQueen Pope's *Give Me Yesterday*; to the Oxford University Press, for quotations from Flora Thompson's *Lark Rise to Candleford* (Oxford University Press, 1945); to Nigel and Benedict Nicolson, Constable and the Hogarth Press, for the quotation from Harold Nicolson's *Small Talk* and Victoria Sackville-West's *The Edwardians*; to Julian Amery, for the quotations from *The Life of Joseph Chamberlain* (Macmillan, 1951); to J. C. Trewin, for the quotation from *The Edwardian Theatre* (Basil Blackwell, 1976); to Alan Delgado, for the quotation from *The Annual Outing and Other Excursions* (George Allen & Unwin, 1977); to Robert Cecil, for the quotation from *Life in Edwardian England* (Batsford, 1969); to Harold Macmillan, for the quotation from *Winds of Change* (Macmillan, 1966); to the Executors of the Estate of the late Mrs. L. B. Masterman for quotations from C. F. G. Masterman's *The Condition of England* (1910); to Isbister Publishers, for the quotation from Jack London's *People of the Abyss* (1902); to Marghanita Laski, Professor Arthur J. Taylor and John Arlott for quotations from their essays in *Edwardian England* (Oxford University Press, 1964, edited by Simon Nowell-Smith); and to the Editor of *The Times*, for extracts from the issues of January 23, 1901, June 5, 1904, May 7, 1910, and two issues in March, 1912.

The author also wishes to express his appreciation to Adrianne LeMan, who designed the book and to Elisabeth Emberson, who researched the pictures and compiled the index, and to Anthony Gould, who devised the series.

FOREWORD
BY SIR CHARLES PETRIE

The reign of King Edward VII, brief as it was, co-incided with the last of Great Britain's prosperous years, and for long there was a not unnatural tendency to regard it as a golden age, much as that of Edward the Confessor was, quite wrongly, regarded by the generation that suffered under the first two Norman sovereigns. We know now that this was not the case, and that the British Empire, in spite of appearances, was passing her zenith when Queen Victoria died; that her commercial and industrial rivals were steadily overtaking her; and the progress of scientific invention was undermining her position as mistress of the seas. While King Edward was still on the throne Blériot flew the Channel, and that was the end of many things, as well as the beginning of many more. All this, how-ever, was hidden from most contemporaries, so that for long there was a tendency to regard King Edward VII and his age in the wrong perspective.

It is well shown in this book that in more than one phase of Edwardian life it was an age of transition, though few contemporaries appear to have noted the fact, and it would seem to have been unrealistic even to suggest that the death of King Edward VII represented a turning-point in the national life of his country. It neither opened the way to free currents, nor diverted the course of those that were already in motion. A new world, which both socially and politi-cally would have been unrecognizable by the great Victorians, had been coming into existence before his accession, and had shown its characteristics strongly enough while he was still on the throne. Moreover, in the last four years of his life domestic politics, culmi-nating in the so-called People's Budget, and foreign affairs, restless and uneasy since the South African War, had already disturbed some men's minds with the sense that the foundations, as well as the surface, of a long familiar world were moving. Whether events, abroad or at home, would have taken a different course had the King lived longer is idle speculation.

Yet in retrospect it is impossible to resist the con-clusion that, even if it be admitted that the year 1910 was no turning-point, it does associate itself with an unwelcome change in the country's state of mind. From such beginnings as serious strikes unauthorized by the Trade Union leaders, the early demonstrations of the new movement for women's suffrage, and the platform extravagances of the 1909 Budget campaign. it grew until a temper of sheer fighting seemed to invade every aspect of affairs. The traditional English-man, with his love of compromise, had become a relic of the past.

The gravest reality was hidden, for the man-in-the-street felt no more than a fatigue in high places, with a hint or two of corruption. Seeing no threat, either political or economic, from without, the mass of the British people thought that they could afford the luxury of quarrelling among themselves, and this they proceeded to do with a bitterness unknown since the late twenties and early thirties of the previous century. But the writing was on the wall, and foreign competit-ion, particularly German, was rapidly becoming a very serious menace.

The events of these years were recorded regularly each week in the pages of *The Illustrated London News,* which had started life early in Queen Victoria's reign as the world's first illustrated weekly newspaper. It was no longer on its own by the time King Edward came to the throne, for the new photographic and printing techniques had already encouraged the launching of the popular daily press, with its emphasis on pictures and large headlines, but *The Illustrated London News* retained its popularity and authority throughout this period, and the pictures reproduced in this book present a powerful portrait of an age which, from whatever angle regarded, was definitely one of transition. Taking all things into consideration, it is impossible to resist the conclusion that of all the changes it initiated, the most revolutionary in every field has proved to be the triumph of the internal com-bustion engine.

1 EDWARD'S KINGDOM

'What will become of the poor country when I die?' questioned Queen Victoria in one of her frequent moments of depression about her son's behaviour. 'If Bertie succeeds he would spend his life in one whirl of amusements.' Brought up with the severity which the Queen believed to be necessary to re-create the image and attitudes of the impeccable Prince Albert, Edward, when Prince of Wales, responded in the refreshingly contrary manner so common in children and grew up decidedly peccable. Queen Victoria's concern was nonetheless misjudged. A man of enormous drive, Edward, as Prince of Wales, was given little opportunity to exercise his energies responsibly. Max Beerbohm's biting caricature depicting 'the rare, the rather awful visits of Albert Edward, Prince of Wales, to Windsor Castle', in which a middle-aged Prince Edward is shown standing in the corner while the elderly Queen sits frowning in the foreground, reflected accurately enough the relationship that so frequently existed between the two. Queen Victoria loved her son, but refused to allow him to grow up and take on many of the royal duties which, as heir to the throne, he had expected and wanted to perform.

The Queen's attitude sprang partly from the loss of her beloved Albert. She could hardly bear the thought, she wrote in her diary, of anyone helping her or 'standing where my dearest had always stood'. She was also jealous of her own position. She informed the Home Secretary that she was against the idea of putting the Prince of Wales forward as the representative of the sovereign: 'Her Majesty thinks it would be most undesirable to constitute the Heir to the Crown a general representative of Herself, and particularly to bring Him forward too frequently before the people. This would necessarily place the Prince of Wales in a position of competing as it were for popularity with the Queen.' The Prince was also refused access to Cabinet papers and Foreign Office despatches, and his requests to the Queen that he be given more official information, instead of having to rely on conversations with friendly ministers and diplomats, were regularly refused, though his requests were occasionally supported by the Prime Minister and the Foreign Secretary. Not until 1886, when Lord Rosebery took over the Foreign Office, did Edward see copies of Foreign Office papers (and then only because Rosebery was a friend), and not until the 1890s, when he was over 50 and clearly getting near to succeeding to the throne, did he receive regular reports of Cabinet meetings similar to those that were given to the Queen.

The Illustrated London News of 1901 recorded the arrival, above, of the new king from Cowes to attend his Accession Council. One of King Edward's first public duties was to open Parliament, which he did in full state, top centre. Queen Alexandra's first public act was to hold a reception at Marlborough House for the Queen Victoria's Institute of Nurses, top right. Later in the year the King returned to Cowes, on board the royal yacht *Osborne*, where ships were dressed to welcome him, right. The visit to Cowes regatta in August was a regular part of the royal year during Edward's reign.

Banished in this way from serious affairs of state, it was perhaps inevitable that so energetic and (as Lord Esher once described him) so *human* a man should have pursued pleasure as an antidote to boredom. He did so with characteristic enthusiasm and determination. His fastidiousness and flair quickly established him as a Prince of fashion, the leader of society and the prime influence of upper class conduct. His own behaviour, though, for one so commonly in the public

eye and so easily recognised (even on his foreign journeys when he sometimes travelled as Baron Renfrew or the Earl of Chester), was on occasion reckless in the extreme, and twice led him into unsavoury court cases. The first occasion was in 1870, when the wife of Sir Charles Mordaunt, MP, told her husband that he was not the father of her child, and named the Prince of Wales (among others), as her lover. Edward gave evidence in the subsequent divorce case, denying that there had been any improper relationship between himself and Lady Mordaunt.

In 1891, Edward found himself in court for the second time. He was called upon to give evidence in an action brought by Lieutenant-Colonel Sir William Gordon Cumming against a group of baccarat players, of whom the Prince was one, who accused him of cheating. Though the verdict went against Gordon Cumming, public opinion, less concerned about the cheating at cards than about the fact that the Prince of Wales should be spending his time gambling, was generally on his side. Edward was, as he had been after the Mordaunt affair, the subject of popular displeasure. He was booed and hissed on some of his public appearances, and he was strongly criticised in the press.

These public revelations of the Prince's unconventional behaviour and dubious associates confirmed the popular reputation of Edward as a prince of pleasure, and certainly strengthened the Queen's resolve not to entrust him with much responsibility. 'The Prince of Wales is not respected' wrote Mr Gladstone, and the Prime Minister's verdict was, at the time, true; it was the penalty paid for the pursuit of pleasure, and in Victorian times not to be respected was a heavy penalty. But the sacrifice of respectability was not accompanied by loss of authority, and it was not permanent. As king, Edward won not only the respect but the love of his people.

When he came to the throne Edward did not abandon his pleasures, nor his old circle of friends — they were, after all, the habits of a life that had already lasted 59 years. But after his accession, on January 22, 1901, Edward became a conscientious sovereign who, in Philip Magnus's happy phrase in his biography of the King (1964), 'made pleasure his servant and not his master'. He was, as far as the monarchy was concerned, a reforming king. He revived pageantry and released the monarchy from many of the restraints that had been put upon it by Victoria. Within a month of the Queen's death he opened Parliament in full state, a ceremony of splendour that had not been seen at Westminster for forty years. He gave Osborne to the Navy for cadet training, though his mother's will had provided for it to be kept in the family. He abandoned

The Boer War was the major national preoccupation at the turn of the century, and it was not finally concluded until 1902. Lord Kitchener, top, negotiated the peace, and its signing was the cause of much rejoicing, including an impromptu bonfire in the streets of Wandsworth, bottom.

Edward's coronation, planned for June, 1902, had to be postponed because of an attack of peritonitis. After the operation for the removal of his appendix anxious crowds gathered outside Buckingham Palace to read the medical bulletins.

Victoria's afternoon 'drawing rooms' in favour of evening courts. He carried out his duties with such enthusiasm, and showed such zest for the occupation of kingship, that both the popularity and prestige of the monarchy were greatly enhanced. Public interest in royalty was revived to such an extent that Lord Northcliffe, in 1908, estimated that the space in newspapers devoted to the movements of royalty had quintupled during his reign.

Publicly expressed doubts about Edward's capacity to be king, put most forcefully by *The Times*, were quickly allayed. In its leading article of January 23, 1901, *The Times* had commented that the new King must often have prayed 'lead us not into temptation' with a feeling akin to hopelessness, and while acknowledging that as Prince he had never failed in his duty to the throne and the nation the newspaper continued, in its heavy Victorian prose, that 'we shall not pretend that there is nothing in his long career which those who respect and admire him would wish otherwise.' But his first acts as King won considerable admiration, and *The Times* and other critics did not remain so

censorious for long. His judgment in deciding to call himself King Edward VII rather than King Albert I, though he had always been known as Bertie, was appreciated, and he established an early authority with his Privy Councillors by his performance at the Accession Council on the second day of his reign, when, on taking the oath of office, he spoke for eight minutes without notes and movingly pronounced his full determination to be a constitutional sovereign in the strictest sense of the word. He proved conscientious in all his kingly duties, less interested perhaps than he might have been in events at home but deeply concerned about foreign affairs and policy, on which he can fairly be said to have been the last English king to have exerted some personal influence.

He was a meticulous reader of official papers, though he often complained that he was not always advised and consulted as much as he should have been when important decisions were being made. In general, however, his complaints on this score met with little sympathy from his Ministers. When, in 1908, he sent through his secretary a request to see a copy of Winston Churchill's war scheme the Prime Minister, Mr Asquith, described the request as 'impertinent' and commented that 'these people have no right to interfere in any way in our deliberations'. Like his mother, Edward never abandoned the claim that it was the sovereign's right to see Cabinet papers while decisions were in process of being made, but Asquith was in fact only following the position taken by Balfour earlier in the reign in refusing to accept that the sovereign had such a right.

It was the general custom throughout the reign, as much demanded by the growing pressure of business as by ministerial feelings of constitutional propriety, to be selective about the political information presented to the sovereign — though he continued to get nightly reports, from either the Prime Minister or his nominee, during parliamentary sessions about the business of the House of Commons. Though these were often entertaining (particularly when, in 1910, Asquith deputed Winston Churchill to write them), they were not the sort of inside information about what the Cabinet was up to that the King was seeking. The perfunctory reports of Cabinet meetings that were sent to the Palace made the King 'an absolute fool', his secretary complained. The King learnt more from his own contacts with ministers and others, but not enough to make him feel that he was properly informed. His irritation on this point no doubt contributed to the difficulty he had in establishing close relations with his Prime Ministers. He had little in common with his Conservative Prime Minister, Arthur Balfour, and not much more with his Liberal

The postponed coronation was held on August 9, 1902, after the King had made a quick recovery from his operation.

The drawing shows the King and Queen returning from Westminster Abbey along St James's Street.

successors, Sir Henry Campbell-Bannerman and
Herbert Henry Asquith.

Neither Campbell-Bannerman nor Asquith was
born into what the King would have recognised as the
ruling group of society, but Campbell-Bannerman
had wealth, which was in the King's view a better
substitute for lineage than the intellectual ability that
Asquith could offer. The King grew to like Campbell-
Bannerman more than he did Asquith, though he was
critical of Campbell-Bannerman's ignorance of foreign
affairs, and when a newspaper photograph showed
King and Prime Minister in close conversation at
Marienbad with the caption 'Is it peace or war?' it was
not surprising that, as the Prime Minister later
revealed, the subject of the earnest conversation turned
out to be whether halibut was better baked or boiled.

His conviction that he was not being adequately
informed did not hinder the King from trying to
influence the course of the nation's affairs with
characteristic forcefulness. At home his major concern
in the early years of his reign was the state of the
armed forces, and he spent so much time with St John
Brodrick, the Secretary of State for War, that the
leader of the Opposition warned Balfour that he might
have to ask a question in the House of Commons about
the constitutional control of the Army. Brodrick himself was later to acknowledge the King's help in

**Coronation illuminations in London, top, as seen from
the top of the campanile of the new Westminster
Cathedral. The study in flags was at Palmerston Road,
Southsea, looking towards Spithead.**

The coronation review at Spithead—the royal yacht passes between the line of naval ships.

reforming the Army and the War Office, and noted in his memoirs that 'the impetus which King Edward gave to all military progress was of abiding service to this country.'

The King also strongly supported the further reforms put into effect by Brodrick's successor, Lord Haldane, for the reorganisation of the Regular Army and for the auxiliary forces — the Militia, Yeomanry and Volunteers. But the passing of the Yeomanry and Reserve Forces Act in 1907, merging the Yeomanry and Volunteers into the Territorial Army, roused such popular resentment that the King feared that not enough young men would come forward to make the experiment successful. Edward was nonetheless tireless in his support, and was always ready to present colours to the new Territorial battalions or to visit their local headquarters, and he did what he could, consistent with constitutional propriety, to make it known that he thought Lloyd George, who was Chancellor of the Exchequer at the time, and Winston Churchill, who was then President of the Board of Trade, were endangering their country's defences by demanding further reductions in the Army Estimates to pay for social benefit schemes.

The King was equally concerned to ensure that the Navy was properly prepared to meet the aggression from abroad which, as his reign progressed, he became more and more convinced was going to come. He gave warm personal support to Admiral Sir John Fisher, who became First Sea Lord in 1904, for the reforms he brought to the Navy — less easily achieved than with the Army, which had suffered the shocks of defeat in the early stages of the Boer War. These reforms included such controversial moves as the introduction of the Dreadnoughts, the new class of warship which had ten 12 inch guns and a speed of 22 knots and the first of which was launched in 1906; the creation of an efficient Reserve Fleet; the scrapping of many old and out-of-date ships; and the formation of a new Home Fleet with a strong complement of battleships.

Fisher was an indiscreet and difficult man whose reforms, though generally right, were introduced with the maximum of confrontation, and he was in the end forced to resign despite the King's support, though he returned to the Admiralty at the outbreak of war in 1914. He remained grateful throughout for the King's help. 'When Your Majesty backed up the First Sea Lord against unanimous Naval feeling against the Dreadnought — when she was first designed — and when Your Majesty launched her, went to sea in her, witnessed her battle practice (which surpassed all records), it just simply shut up the mouths of the revilers as effectively as those lions were kept from eating Daniel!' he wrote in 1907. 'And they would have eaten me but for Your Majesty!' On learning of the King's death three years later Fisher wrote that he had 'conquered all hearts and annihilated all envy'.

The King's natural interest in foreign affairs, his anxiety about the state of Europe, his frequent and regular visits abroad and his personal acquaintance with so many rulers and political leaders earned him a very high reputation both at home and abroad as a diplomat and international statesman. He was described by the Italian Foreign Minister as 'the arbiter of Europe's destiny, the most powerful personal factor in world policy', and by the United States Ambassador in London as 'the greatest mainstay of peace in Europe'. His influence in the field of foreign affairs was undoubtedly exaggerated. Bernard Shaw, who was at the height of his powers during the Edwardian era, once said that kings were not born, but made by universal hallucination. In Edward's case the hallucination, which led to the French giving him the title of 'l'Oncle de l'Europe' following his triumphant visit to Paris in 1903, was certainly as common in Europe as it was in Britain. The King naturally enjoyed his reputation, but he was under no illusion that he possessed the power with which he was credited. He believed in the British Government's policy of establishing *ententes cordiales* with France and with Russia, and because successive British Governments were shy of advertising their policies, knowing that they were unpopular with the British electorate, while he was not, the King was able to play an effective role in preparing opinion, both in Britain and in Europe, for the working out of new policies. His success in this public relations activity made him seem, at times, indeed to be the arbiter of Europe.

That he was not in reality able to exercise such authority was always evident to him, and towards the end of his life he became increasingly depressed by the prospect of war in Europe. His attempts to reassure the Kaiser that Britain's moves towards France and Russia had no aggressive intent towards Germany were not wholly successful in spite of his persistence. The two men met frequently but found it hard to maintain the co-operative spirit they enjoyed at the beginning of Edward's reign, when the Kaiser, on the last day of his visit to attend Queen Victoria's

Shooting stags in the Balmoral deer forest. Shooting was one of the King's favourite sports, and remained so throughout his life.

The King was a keen racegoer, and seldom lost an opportunity of visiting a course, particularly when one of his own horses was running, as at Kempton Park in February, 1903, top. In 1909 the King's career as an owner reached its peak when his horse *Minoru*, bottom, won the Derby.

Right, on the Sunday of Ascot week the crowds amused themselves on the river. This was the colourful and elegant scene at Boulter's Lock in July, 1901.

funeral, spoke of the need to form an Anglo-German alliance: 'You would watch over the seas while we would safeguard the land,' the Kaiser said. 'With such an alliance, not a mouse would stir in Europe.'

Six months later, when he went to Germany to attend his sister's funeral, the King made one of his few diplomatic gaffes when he impulsively handed to the Kaiser confidential notes on Anglo-German relations provided for him by the British Foreign Secretary, Lord Lansdowne. Fortunately the notes contained nothing to upset the Kaiser, though they afforded him some amusement at the expense of the British Foreign Office because of an elementary error of geography. Though King and Kaiser continued to meet their relationship deteriorated when Germany tried to engineer a crisis over Morocco into a means of torpedoing the alliance with France, and neither man trusted the other. The King returned from his final visit to Germany in 1909 in low spirits and looking tired and ill.

His depression was only partly caused by his fear of war with Germany. He was also out of sympathy with the social reforms which the Liberal Government was introducing, and which he believed threatened the established order of society. He saw the same dangers in the growth of the suffragette movement, and in the dispute between the two Houses of Parliament and the demands for the reform of the Lords following the rejection of the 'People's Budget' brought in by Lloyd George in 1909. The House of Lords rejected the King's advice when it threw out the Finance Bill, and the King was thus faced with the prospect of having to agree to create several hundred Liberal peers, an act which would, he believed, cause irreparable damage to the House of Lords and seriously affect the position of the Crown. Not for the first time during these last years of his reign, he talked of abdication. The constitutional crisis had not been resolved when, on Friday May 6, 1910, King Edward collapsed and died of a series of heart attacks.

The outburst of popular grief that followed the announcement of his death was indicative of the remarkable affection he had inspired among his own people, and indeed among others. *The Times*, so critical at the time of his accession, now published a leader entitled 'The Sorrow of the World' in which it noted with astonishment the intensity of world sympathy. 'Never in our long history', wrote *The Times,* 'has any sorrow of ours been more deeply and more generally felt than the death of King Edward . . . All bear witness to the greatness of his Kingly qualities, to the wisdom of his statesmanship, to the lovableness of his personal character, and to his unwearying care for the welfare and the interests of

The King was a regular visitor to Marienbad. The drawing by Matania, above, shows him on his daily visit to the springs.

Top right, the King and the Tsar of Russia and their families in Cowes, 1909.

Bottom right, the King with a shooting party at Chatsworth in 1907. On the left is Mrs Keppel.

his people.' Lord Morley, then Secretary of State for India, noted that 'the feeling of grief and the sense of personal loss throughout the country, indeed through-

out Western Europe, is extraordinary.'

The Edwardian age did not long survive the King. It was a questioning age, when it was no longer possible to assume, as Victorians had, that Britain was the richest and most powerful nation in the world, and the pomp and circumstance that Edward gave to the monarchy provided some focus of reassurance. Meticulous as he was about the formalities of diplomatic procedure and court etiquette, he was inclined to be indulgent in other things, as he was so frequently indulgent to himself. But in spite of escapades in foreign watering-places, and many affairs closer to home, Edward preserved a happy family life and was a devoted husband and father — a situation which did not seem as contradictory in Edwardian times as it may do today, and was certainly not uncommon. It was his wife, Queen Alexandra, who sent for Mrs Alice Keppel when it was learnt that the King was dying. To his subjects King Edward seemed, as J. B. Priestley wrote in *The Edwardians* (1970), 'a typical Englishman with the lid off'. His presence always created an atmosphere that was exhilarating. 'He wanted everyone around him to be happy', wrote Philip Magnus, 'and, though faultlessly attired, he encouraged friends' children to race slices of hot buttered toast for pennies along the stripes of his trousers, with the buttered side downwards, and to call him "Kingy" in the privacy of their parents' homes.' His ability to put people at their ease was not confined to friends and family. Once, when entertaining an Indian prince to dinner at Buckingham Palace he noticed that his guest was throwing his asparagus stalks onto the carpet. The King at once began to do the same. 'He had just the character', wrote Lord Morley, 'that Englishmen thoroughly understand, thoroughly like . . . He combined regal dignity with *bonhomie*, and strict regard for form with entire absence of spurious pomp.'

The events that followed the King's death were to show how much his force of character had served as a bridge between the stability of the nineteenth century and the restlessness of the twentieth. The era that he personified was not just a pendant to the Victorian age, nor simply a brief prelude to the revolutionary epoch that was to follow. It was a short but distinctive age of transition in which the King's own personality and behaviour reflected with surprising accuracy the generation that grew out of the Victorian age with him. The four years that immediately followed his death saw the spread of syndicalism, strikes, social unrest, militant suffragettes, the threat of civil war in Ireland — events which, if they tended to obscure the onrush of war, were finally engulfed by it, as was so much of the old order, just as King Edward had feared.

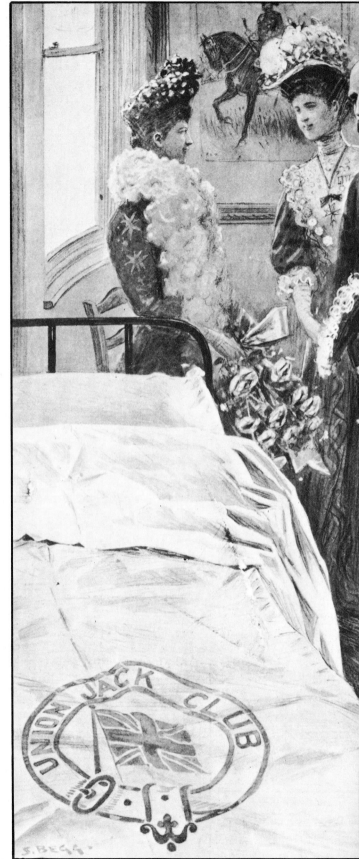

Left, the Union Jack Club for soldiers and sailors was opened by King Edward in 1907. The drawing shows the King inspecting a bedroom for which he had himself provided the money.

Above, during a visit to the National Hospital for the Paralysed and Epileptic, the King submitted himself to electric shock. The King was a keen supporter of medical research, once writing that his greatest ambition was "not to quit this world till a real cure for cancer has been found".

Top, Professor Sir William Ramsay, discoverer of inert gases, in conference about his experiments with Professor Pierre Curie, who with his wife Marie had discovered radium.

Bottom, a cinematograph display of bacilli at the King's College Hospital Medical Society.

Centre, at the Royal Society in 1909 a bulldog named Jimmy had his heartbeats recorded by electricity.

Far right (top), the first motor lawn mower was demonstrated in 1905.

Far right (bottom), advertisements for a portable shower bath and an electric torch (1902), and the Kinora picture animator (1903).

Above, the *Discovery* leaving New Zealand on her way to the Antarctic in 1901, with Captain Scott in command. Scott returned to the region 10 years later, reaching the South Pole with four companions in January, 1912, to find that Amundsen's Norwegian expedition had already been there. Scott and his men perished on their way back.

Top right, the launch of what was then, in 1906, the biggest battleship in the world, HMS *Dreadnought*. Bottom right, in 1901 the largest liner in the world was the White Star ship *Celtic*, 20,880 tons, but she was soon to be surpassed in both size and speed.

2 TOWN LIFE

The industrial explosion of the Victorian era transformed Britain from a rural into an urban society, and
that dramatic change was rapidly and permanently
consolidated during the reign of Edward VII. Though
at the time of his death only 8 per cent of the population worked on the land, he was himself more familiar
with an England that had its roots in the country.
Society was still dominated by the traditions of the
landed aristocracy and politics by men who for the
most part derived their position from the fact that
they owned land. But the nation's wealth was earned
in the towns, by means of trade and industry, and the
men who practised these occupations were beginning
to exert their influence in government as in other
fields. It was economic necessity that forced the
majority of Edward's subjects into the towns. The
importing of cheap food from America and elsewhere
made it impossible to grow food economically in
England, with the result that the flow of agricultural
workers to the towns continued, and although the
creation of more smallholdings by the Liberal Government of 1906 put some check on the process (the
census of 1911 recorded an increase in the total of
farm labourers for the first time in more than 50 years),
by 1911 less than a quarter of the total population of
40 million lived on the land.

The towns were ill-prepared to receive this invasion
of the less fortunate of the rural population, in spite
of the ostentatious show of affluence which has tended
to colour accounts of Edwardian England as some
departed 'golden age'. Because of the emphasis on
trade, shipping and overseas investment, the increase
in wealth during this period was centred largely on
London, where some 5,000,000 people lived. Statistics
for the distribution of national wealth at the start of
Edward's reign show that out of a total population of
some 33,000,000, less than 1,000,000 were liable to
pay income tax which, at the rate of one shilling in the
pound, was levied on incomes of £160 a year or more,
and no more than 400,000 people declared their
incomes at more than £400 a year. Only a com-
paratively few, therefore, enjoyed wealth, but enjoy it
they certainly did. They formed a small proportion of
the population, but they stamped their image on their
times. It was they — popularly categorised at the time
as the 'idle rich' — who provided the glitter and the

**A dinner for the London poor was given by the King at
Bishop's Park, Fulham, where there were, according to
contemporary reports of the occasion, at least half a
million guests.**

gaiety, the style and the extravagance, the flamboyant fashion and the parties till dawn, that tend to dominate reminiscences of the years between the start of the century and the coming of the First World War — memories that have been coloured, perhaps, by the awful contrast that war provided for those who survived it and could remember with nostalgia the period before Western civilisation turned upon itself. But to describe them as 'idle rich' is not strictly accurate, for though their wealth was undeniable, and very visible, they were certainly not idle. Even those who had no useful work to do found ways of keeping themselves frantically occupied simply keeping up with fashion and society, which proved, as J. B. Priestley has recalled, ferocious taskmasters:

'To keep in, to keep going, members of Edwardian high society toiled harder than overworked clerks or warehousemen. It was a dreadful nuisance, of course, but a fellow would have to go down to Cowes for the first week in August, then go up North to shoot the grouse or stalk the deer. A woman invited for a weekend at one of the great houses would have to take several large trunks, and then would have to be changing clothes — and always looking at her best — half-a-dozen times a day. A free-and-easy life in theory, in practice it was more highly disciplined and more wearing than the life of a recruit in the Life Guards.'

The King himself set the pace. He could not bear to be unoccupied, and as Prince of Wales, when there were not too many demands on his time, he had established an intricate routine to keep himself on the move, and he stuck to the same pattern when he became King. His routine was to spend Christmas and the New Year at Sandringham, moving to Buckingham Palace in January in time for the State Opening of Parliament. He maintained an active social life while in London, either entertaining or going to dinner or theatre parties every night. In March he left England for two months, usually to spend a short time in Paris, several weeks in Biarritz and several more cruising in the Mediterranean. He would return to London at the beginning of May for the Season, when he would again dine out or entertain every night. In the middle of June he would move to Ascot for the races and then, after a visit to some provincial town for a few days in July, would stay with the Duke of Richmond for the racing at Goodwood before taking up residence on board the royal yacht for the regatta at Cowes. After this he would take a month's cure at Marienbad. Returning to London in September, the King would spend a week or two at Buckingham Palace before going up to Balmoral, for the grouse and deer, where he stayed throughout October, except for a trip down

Above, the Prince of Wales visiting new tenements at 57 Cadogan House, Chelsea, in which the rents ranged from 3s 6d to 7s a week.

Right, two sides of London life: Top, high society dining at Dieudonne's, in St James's; bottom, the "flotsam and jetsam" of London, as they were described in *The Illustrated London News* of the time, having been moved out of Hyde Park, ended up in the hour before dawn at Shepherd's Bush Green.

to the Newmarket races in the royal train. The end of the year would be divided between Windsor, Sandringham and Buckingham Palace, and would culminate in a whirl of Christmas parties at which the eating would be more relentless than ever.

Food was more than a necessity for Edwardian society; it was also a major pastime. The King, again, set a formidable example. His own dinners generally comprised at least twelve courses, and he was particularly fond of dishes like pheasant stuffed with snipe or woodcock, with the latter stuffed in its turn with truffles, and the whole covered with some rich sauce. He also ate hearty breakfasts, lunches, teas (at which his normal fare was lobster salad) and suppers. So, too, did his subjects, or those who could afford it.

Heavy eating was a characteristic of the Edwardian era. Sir Charles Petrie, in *Scenes of Edwardian Life* (1965), has published the menu of a dinner given by his father, when Lord Mayor of Liverpool, in 1902 in honour of Lord Rosebery:

Caviar   Anchois

———

Tortue Claire

———

Saumon, Sauce Medoc   Filet de Sole à l'Adelphi

———

Poulet, Reine Demidoff   Asperge en Branches au Beurre

———

Quartier d'Agneau

———

Filet de Boeuf Hollandaise

———

Granit au Kummel

———

Canard Sauvage   Bécasses   Russian Salad

———

Pouding Imperial   Macedoine au Fruits
Meringue au Crème

———

Pouding Glace à la Chantilly

———

Dessert

Edwardian recipe books suggest that even at home dieting was not of much concern, and of course the King was not the only one to take a cure regularly.

The 1906 edition of Mrs Beeton's *Book of Household Management* suggests that anything from a four to a six course meal would be normal for an upper or middle class family dining alone, and far more elaborate meals would be produced when the family was entertaining — even for breakfast. Here is Mrs Beeton's suggestion for a 'simple' breakfast suitable for large parties:

Oatmeal Porridge
Kidney Omelet
Baked eggs (au gratin)
Fried Cod
Grilled Ham
Potted Game
Veal Cake
Stewed Prunes and Cream
Scones, Rolls, Toast, Bread
Butter, Marmalade, Jam
Tea, Coffee, Cream, Milk

Indulgence in food was accompanied by strict discipline in fashion. Gentlemen wore frock-coats and top-hats during the day, ladies wore long skirts, tightly laced corsets and enormous hats. If she went

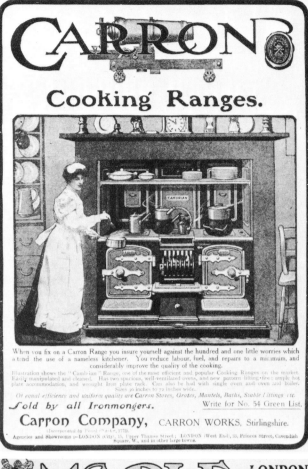

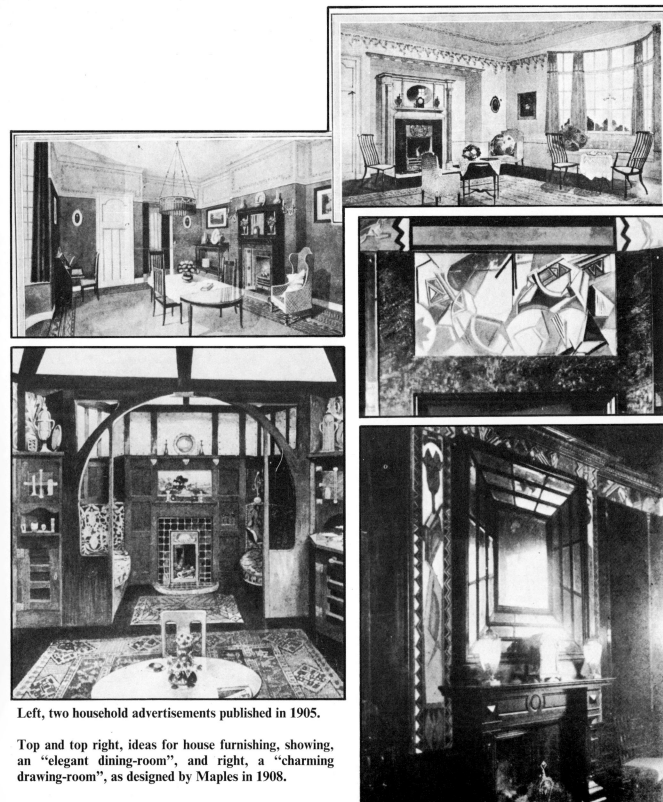

Left, two household advertisements published in 1905.

Top and top right, ideas for house furnishing, showing, an "elegant dining-room", and right, a "charming drawing-room", as designed by Maples in 1908.

Above, fashionable ingle-nook, 1904. Right, "futurist" designs in house furnishing taken from Lady Drogheda's town house in Wilton Crescent in 1914. The frieze over the door was designed by Wyndham Lewis.

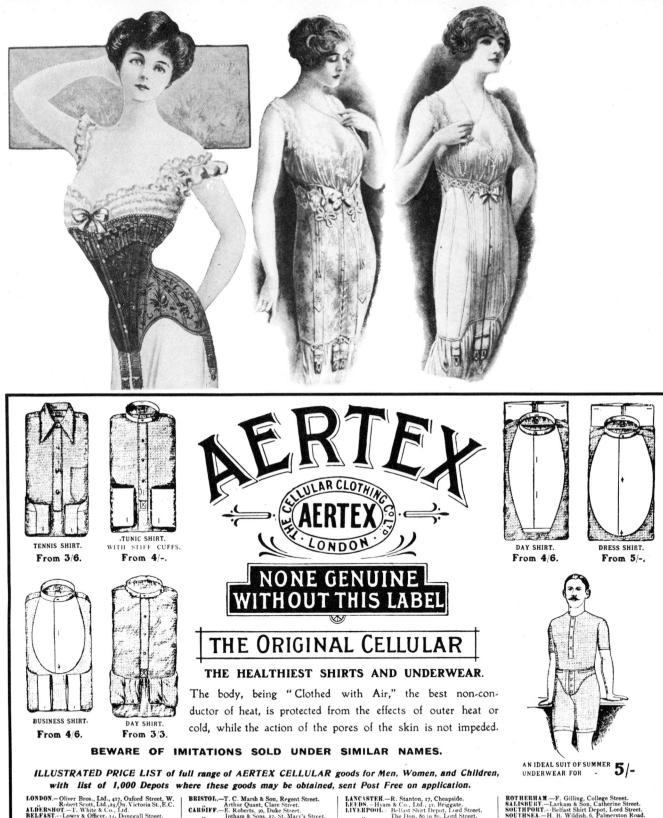

Corsets were the foundation of Edwardian fashion, and *The Illustrated London News* of the period carried advertisements, top left, for a variety of models, including the "Imperial", left, the "Nature", right, and the "Thigh-Diminishing", centre. Men also were catered for in the advertisement section of the magazine, as the "Aertex" announcement for "the healthiest shirts and underwear", left, shows.

Above, a smart bathing-gown. Top right, tailored gown trimmed with silver braid, and far right, severely-cut hobble skirt. Right, the *bonnet d'ane*, or donkey's-ears hat, which was the vogue in 1913.

riding in Rotten Row, a lady rode side-saddle, though she was no longer required to conceal the fact that she had ankles. Fashions varied, though not very dramatically, during the reign: coats and skirts were now being worn by ladies, as well as by 'working women', and the length of the skirt moved up and down — though never up very far. Edward introduced the Homburg and the Norfolk jacket, among other fashions for men, though his occasional habit of having his trousers creased sideways never caught on. In general, however, everyone in society conformed with a fairly rigid convention in dress, and was made to feel uncomfortable if he did not. Sir Frederick Ponsonby, who was the King's Assistant Private Secretary, was witheringly rebuked when he proposed to accompany his master in a tail-coat to an exhibition of pictures one morning: 'I thought everyone must know', said the King, 'that a short jacket is always worn with a silk hat at a private view in the morning.'

The standard of living of the well-to-do was dependent partly on the low rate of income tax, but perhaps even more on the plentiful supply of domestic servants. 'Service' was much the largest field of employment for women. Of 4,000,000 women employed at the beginning of Edward's reign 1,500,000 were in domestic service. By 1911 the number had

increased to over 2,000,000. In that year a total of 2,600,000 men and women were employed as servants, most of them in the towns. Today there are not much more than 100,000.

The census of 1901 had used the phrase 'standard of comfort', which it defined as the number of domestic servants employed for every hundred separate occupiers or families. The 'standard of comfort' varied greatly from one part of the country to another. In parts of London, for example, there were twelve menservants and eighty female domestics for every hundred occupiers; in Rochdale there were no menservants and only seven women. In every rich middle class household the servants were a stable and rigidly hierarchical society, with a settled career pattern. Women began as a between-maid, or tweenie, at around £12 a year and advanced to head housemaid at up to £30, or from scullery maid to cook or cook-housekeeper, who might earn as much as £80. The lowest rung of the ladder for a man was page, or buttons, who would start at about £10 a year, and who would if he were diligent and fortunate advance to the top rung, when he would become butler, earning perhaps £100 a year.

Well-ordered and stable though it was, there were signs even in Edwardian times that life behind the green baize door was changing. The signs were most

Left, summer fashions on display at the Ranelagh Club in Barnes. Above, a sack-race for wearers of hobble-skirts or "tube" frocks, as they were described in 1910. Right, the jupe-culotte drew the disapproval of *The Illustrated London News* in 1911, which headed this picture "inelegance" and noted that its wearers, however satisfied they might be with the freedom it gave to their limbs, found it mentally uncomfortable because of the "active curiosity" it aroused.

apparent in the households of the middle classes, where the servants were fewer and less well disciplined. Mrs C. S. Peel, who in 1902 wrote a book entitled *How to Keep House*, which is quoted in Marghanita Laski's chapter on domestic life in *Edwardian Life* (1964), described the difficulties: 'The young working-girl of today prefers to become a Board School mistress, a post-office clerk, a typewriter, a shop girl, or a worker in a factory — anything rather than enter domestic service.' Mrs Peel did not blame the girls, who were intent, she said, on becoming young ladies. But she had some hard words for the house-hold manager. 'Mistresses', she said, 'are no longer interested in their craft. They despise and know nothing of housekeeping and fail to train their daughters to run a home.'

With taxes so low life for the middle classes was comfortable and secure; the majority lived within their incomes and were able to provide something for their descendants. Even in London the cost of living was not high, and prices stayed stable during most of Edward's reign. A small house in a fashionable part of London might be rented for about £200 a year, and a small staff of three or four to run it would cost less than half this amount. The income of a reasonably well set up middle class family might be £2,000. Miss Laski quotes the annual budget of such a family which lived near London, comprising a husband, wife, three daughters aged fourteen, sixteen and eighteen, and two sons who were already in business and needed only small allowances, as follows:

	£
Rent, rates and taxes	300
Boys' allowances @ £50 each	100
Governess and classes for girls	100
Dress and personal allowances for husband and wife @ £100 each	200
Wine	50
Coal and light	45
Wages (manservant £50, cook £30, kitchenmaid £16, 2 housekeepers @ £20 and £16, sewing-maid £25)	157
Washing @ £2 a week	104
Housebills for 14 people	437
Garden and stable expenses (including wages of 2 men and 1 boy and keep of 2 cobs)	300
	—
Total	£1,793

It is reasonable to conclude from these figures that, apart from the service provided, no very extravagant living could have been possible. The family holidays, which had to come from the £207 left after payment of all the above expenses, could hardly amount to more than a brief period at a seaside resort. The sum provided for the girls would have been insufficient to send the girls to one of the good new boarding-schools like Roedean where, in the uniform jibbahs and cloaks, they could enjoy such amenities as the swimming-pool, the carpentry shop, the domestic science wing, and the splendid playing fields for hockey and lacrosse, cricket and tennis.

There were of course many rising middle class families who lived contentedly on incomes much lower than £2,000 a year. Many moved away from the ill-kept town centres into the suburbs, for the new and more rapid methods of transport brought a great

Whist drives became a suburban craze in 1909, and led to many marriages, according to *The Illustrated London News*, which reported that but for whist "many girls who have little opportunity of meeting the opposite sex would remain spinsters".

spread of suburban development in Edwardian times. The word suburbia had been coined in the last decade of Queen Victoria's reign, when counties such as Middlesex, Essex and Surrey had recorded large population increases, but it was in the years that followed that the edges of the inner cities were filled in with such solidity — areas such as West Ham, Willesden, Hornsey and Tottenham round London, King's Norton and Smethwick round Birmingham, and Wallasey in Liverpool. The rows of redbrick terraced houses in these city suburbs became characteristic of Edwardian building, reproducing the town, as *The Times* commented in June 1904, 'in its least interesting or stimulating form'. A house in an inner suburb of London might be bought for under £1,000 and rents were not high. A six-roomed house in an inner suburb such as Edmonton or Clapham (called the 'capital of Suburbia' by one contemporary critic) could be rented for less than £1, perhaps no more than 10s a week. It was into these areas that the rapidly growing class of white-collar workers moved, men and women with some education who were meeting the need for clerks and bookkeepers in business and commerce. The advantages that the suburbs brought — cleaner air, more light, a garden, escape perhaps from unsuitable neighbours regarded as inferior —

The first completed section of electric tramways in West London was inaugurated in carnival style in July, 1901. Above right, automatic slot-machines for penny stamps were introduced by the Post Office in 1907.

Giles Gilbert Scott's design for Liverpool Cathedral, one of the most distinguished Edwardian buildings.

The pedestrian tunnel under the Thames between Greenwich and Millwall was opened in August, 1902. The tunnel, which took three years to build, was 1,217 feet long and had an inside diameter of 35 feet.

were accompanied by some disadvantages. In his book *The Condition of England*, published in 1909, C. F. G. Masterman suggested that while they succeeded in winning 'the struggle to live', they too often led to the pursuit of false values in 'the struggle to attain'. Though children grew healthy, the mental climate was enervating. There was increasing separation of different classes in different localities — the working classes in the slums, the lower middle classes in the inner suburbs, the middle classes in the outer suburbs — with the result that contact, and social conscience, was dissipated.

The growth of suburbia depended on transport, which made rapid advances during this period, particularly in and around the towns. For long-distance transport the railway remained supreme, and railway traffic increased yearly. Within the towns the revolutionary changes were caused by the spread of trams, buses and, in London, the underground railway. Electric trams had been first introduced into provincial cities in the 1890s, and they came to London in the first year of the new century. They replaced the horse buses and trams, and proved faster, cheaper and capable of going farther. The mileage of tramways in Britain was doubled in the first seven years of the century, but by the end of Edward's reign the tram network was already beginning to be undermined by the development of reliable motor buses. The London General Omnibus Company developed its 'B' type bus in 1910, and by 1913 there were some three thousand motor buses on the streets of London. They did not develop without opposition, however, being strongly criticised for their noise and smell, and for the destruction they caused — by 1912 buses were running people over at the rate of nearly two hundred a year. Few cars travelled in towns at the beginning of Edward's reign, private motoring still being regarded as a hobby for the rich — though the first introduction of the cheap Ford motor cars from America in 1908 heralded the motoring age that was to develop later in the century. Hansom cabs and open or closed carriages were the recognised means of transport for

Oxford Circus underground station, on what was then called the Baker Street and Waterloo Tube Railway, was opened in 1906. The last of the new underground lines, Hampstead, became operational in the following year.

those whose pocket did not force them to use horse buses or trams. The first motor taxi-cabs appeared on the streets of London in 1903, and by 1910 they outnumbered horse-drawn cabs by 6,300 to 5,000. By 1914 the streets of London had been dramatically changed by the development of motorised public transport, though the road surfaces were only slowly improved to meet the increase of traffic upon them.

Changes on the surface were accompanied by equally revolutionary developments underground. The first underground railway, the Metropolitan Line, had been opened in London in 1863. This was a steam-engined railway, and the experience of working with these trains was vividly described by a young railwayman who joined the District Railway in 1901 and quoted in W. MacQueen Pope's book *Give Me Yesterday*:

'In the tunnels, steam and sulphur were the order of the day. The locomotives were small and powerful. They had no cab, only a weatherboard, therefore the driver and fireman were exposed to the elements when

they left the tunnels. Blackfriars station was the place for steam and sulphur! It seemed to cling there. Gower Street on the Metropolitan was its rival. The traffic in those days was very heavy in the rush hours and almost as heavy all the day. The celebrations on Ladysmith Day, Mafeking Night, during Queen Victoria's funeral and Edward VII's Coronation called for the moving of many thousands of people. They moved in safety by steam trains.'

The Illustrated London News of April 11, 1903, reported the findings of an inquiry promoted by the London County Council into the air to be found in the Central London Railway tube. In the morning, when the tube had been ventilated, it was noted that the air was 'of fair purity'. As the day passed, however, the amount of carbonic acid ('or Carbon dioxide, as chemists term it') exceeded the amount found in the 'outer atmosphere' (ie above ground). And with regard to germs, it was found that the number was slightly higher in the air of the tube than in the outside air; but the report added that 'the railway might

* "London's new amusement: up and down the escalator" was the heading over this drawing of the revolutionary moving staircase at Earls Court station in 1911. Passengers were asked not to sit on the stairs, and to step off with the left foot first.

Right, sectional views of the Earls Court escalator were published to show how it worked, and to reassure the public that it was safe to travel on, a man with a wooden leg was hired to go up and down to demonstrate its safety.

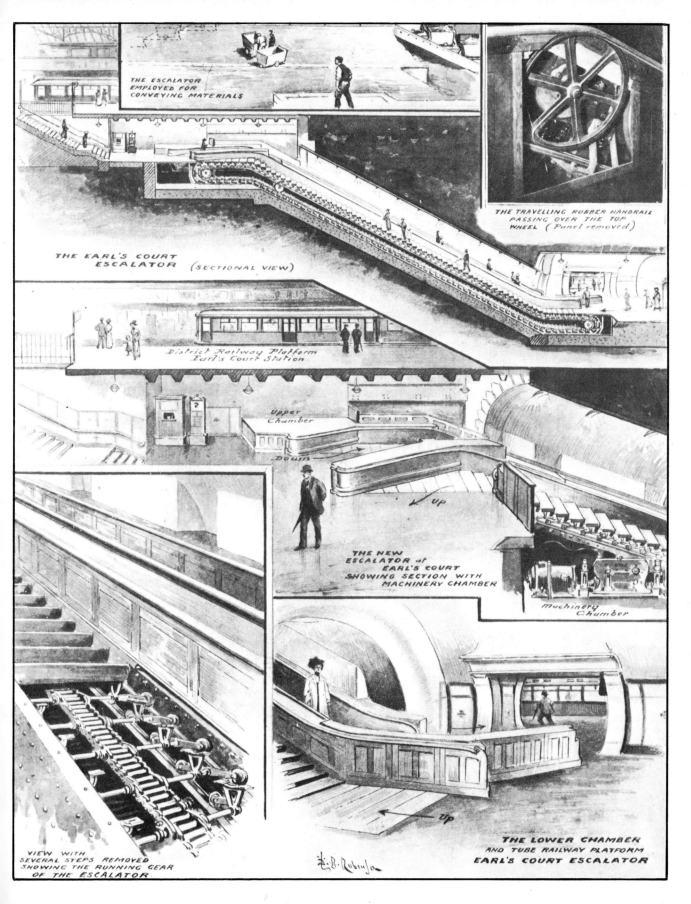

THE ESCALATOR EMPLOYED FOR CONVEYING MATERIALS

THE TRAVELLING RUBBER HANDRAIL PASSING OVER THE TOP WHEEL (Panel removed)

THE EARL'S COURT ESCALATOR (SECTIONAL VIEW)

District Railway Platform
Earl's Court Station

Upper Chamber

Down

Up

THE NEW ESCALATOR at EARL'S COURT SHOWING SECTION WITH MACHINERY CHAMBER

Machinery Chamber

VIEW WITH SEVERAL STEPS REMOVED SHOWING THE RUNNING GEAR OF THE ESCALATOR

Up

THE LOWER CHAMBER AND TUBE RAILWAY PLATFORM
EARL'S COURT ESCALATOR

compare very favourably with the conditions that are represented, say, in small living rooms, where the cubic space is limited and the ventilation deficient.' The *ILN* questioned whether, in fact, the dangers in the tube were any greater than those in places of amusement, churches and halls where large numbers of people assembled. The important thing, the magazine declared, was that the public mind 'be awakened to the necessity for fresh air as a paramount condition of a healthy existence'.

The District Line railwayman quoted above also recalled the introduction of electrification, which began in the 1890s and greatly improved the atmosphere in the tubes:

'An experimental train operated between Earls Court and High Street, Kensington. We did not think much of it. The Central London Railway from the Bank to Shepherd's Bush opened in 1900 as The Tuppenny Tube — fare twopence anywhere on the line. The early trains were hauled by electric locomotives but the vibration was so great that they had to be abandoned for the present type of central-equipped passenger car. The Eastern terminus of the District Railway was Whitechapel and in 1902 the Bow Line was opened. It connected the District Railway with the London, Tilbury and Southend Railway. The line had three stations, Stepney Green, Mile End and Bow Road, which gave a through line from Ealing Broadway or Hounslow Barracks to Southend. The stations started a building boom along that fifty miles of track. Ealing Broadway was a semi-country station, during the day two trains per hour to London. There was a large bell on the platform roof which the ticket collector rang three minutes before the train was due to leave. As he rang, he would say, "Let's see who's got 'eart disease." Ealing was populated by many retired people, Indian Civil Servants, retired officers etc, many of the very old school, white side-whiskers, bandy legs, plum-coloured nose and face and a Bangalore liver. I am glad I saw them. Their like will not come again. When a Levée was held at St James's we saw many of the officers of the Indian Army in review order — uniforms we could not identify.'

In 1907 the Hampstead Tube was opened, and this proved to be the last new line to become operational until 1969, when the Victoria Line opened. The moving staircase, though invented, was not brought into common use in underground stations before the First World War, though one was installed at Earls Court station in 1911 — it aroused such mistrust that a man with a wooden leg had to be hired to go up and down it to demonstrate its safety. The underground, more than the tram or the motor bus because it could go farther and faster more cheaply, provided many

The Edwardian period saw the construction of many large shops in Oxford Street. One of the first, above, was Waring and Gillow, the construction of whose Galleries of Furniture and Applied Decorative Art was completed in 1905. Right, three years later work began on Selfridge's, which was to become London's biggest shop and "a wonder of commercial enterprise".

Two early twentieth-century buildings: Westminster Cathedral shortly before its completion in the first year of Edward's reign, and, bottom, design for the London County Council offices, on the south side of Westminster Bridge, whose construction began in 1912.

The Victoria and Albert Museum. Begun in 1899, the building was completed in 1909, and opened that year by the King.

Ten years after Queen Victoria had laid the foundation-stone of the Victoria and Albert Museum, King Edward

received the key to the £1 million building from the Commissioner of Works.

Londoners with the opportunity not just to get away from the city for a day, but to commute every night and every weekend. To escape the squalor of the city centres the middle and lower middle classes commuted to the suburbs in increasing numbers; but there were many left behind who were too poor to escape.

Between 1871 and 1911 the population of Greater London rose from 3,890,000 to 7,256,000. The result of this near doubling was more than uncomfortable. Houses vacated by the middle classes were being divided up to provide accommodation for the rural immigrants, and once respectable districts were degenerating into slums. In Edwardian census reports overcrowding was officially defined as an average of more than two persons to a room; by that standard more than 8 per cent of the total population of England and Wales was overcrowded during the Edwardian period. In the East End of London the proportion of people living more than two to a room was more than 30 per cent, in Glasgow it was 59 per cent. In such areas the three-relay system was often standard practice — each bed being let to three tenants, who had the right to occupy it for an eight-hour shift, so that the bed was never empty. More often than not the space below the bed would be similarly let. Jack London, the American journalist and novelist, reported on the state of one room he saw in the East End:

'It was not a room . . . It was a den, a lair. Seven feet by eight were its dimensions, and the ceiling was so low as not to give the cubic airspace required by a British soldier in barracks. A crazy couch, with ragged coverlets, occupied nearly half the room. A rickety table, a chair, and a couple of boxes left little space in which to turn around . . . The floor was bare, while the walls and ceilings were literally covered with blood marks and splotches. Each mark represented a violent death — of an insect, for the place swarmed with vermin.' In 1901 B. Seebohm Rowntree, in his book *Poverty, a Study of Town Life,* gave this description of a house in York:

'Two rooms. Seven inmates. Walls, ceiling and furniture filthy. Dirty flock bedding in living-room placed on a box and two chairs. Smell of room from dirt and bad air unbearable, and windows and doors closed. There is no through ventilation in this house. Children pale, starved-looking and only half clothed. One boy with hip disease, another with sores all over face.' A

Jewish immigrants fleeing from Europe aggravated conditions in England's overcrowded cities. Some paused in London or Hull on their way to America, others strove to earn a living in sweatshops such as this tailor's den in the East End of London.

report from HM Commissioners inquiring into the conditions of the working classes at this time stated that overcrowding was a greater cause of deterioration of health than were infectious diseases.

In his study of York Rowntree defined a poverty line for the basic financial requirements for food, rent, and other essentials. He set the figures at 7s a week for a single man, 21s 8d for a family comprising husband, wife, and three children, and 37s 4d for a family of husband, wife, and eight children. He estimated that 27·8 per cent of the population of York, and 43·4 per cent of the city's wage earners, were living in poverty. Rowntree also gave a typical week's purchases for the family of a York labourer earning 17s 6d a week, the family comprising husband, wife and five children, the eldest of whom was deformed and threatened with tuberculosis, while the others showed clear signs of deprivation:

Friday: 1½st flour, 1s 10½d. ¼st wheatmeal, 4d. Yeast, 1d. 1lb butter, 10d. 2½lb bacon, 1s. 6oz tea, 6d. 1lb currants, 3d. 1lb lard, 4d. 1½lb fish, 4d. 1 tin condensed milk, 5½d. Onions, 1d.

Saturday: Bag of coal, 1s 3d. 4lb beef, 1s 7½d. 5lb sugar, 9d. ½lb dripping, 2½d. ½st potatoes, 2d. 8 eggs, 6d. Baking powder, 1d. Literature, 2d. 1oz tobacco, 3d. Black lead, 1d. Lemons, 2d. Cabbage, 2d. Insurance 5d.

Sunday: Milk, 1d.

Monday: Stamp, 1d. Stationery, 1d. Sewing-cotton, 2d. Glycerine, 2d. Pair of slippers, 1s 1½d. Rent, 3s 3d.

Tuesday: Yeast, 1d. 1lb. soap, 2¼d. Starch, 1d. Blacking, 1d. Scrubbing brush, 3½d.

Wednesday: Nothing.

Thursday: Lettuce, 1d.

The diet provided by these purchases was, as Rowntree noted, 'very inadequate'.

There were many worse off, who nonetheless contrived to earn something, even if it was less than 17s 6d a week. And there were others who had dropped out of the system altogether. These were the outcasts of Edwardian society, of whom it was estimated there were some 35,000 in London, condemned to walk the streets all night ('carrying the banner' as it was called) and quickly moved on by the police if they fell asleep in a public place. Jack London joined them one night:

'Among those who carry the banner, Green Park has the reputation of opening its gates earlier than the other parks, and at quarter past four in the morning, I and many more entered Green Park. It was raining again, but they were worn out with the night's walking,

and they were down on the benches and asleep at once.'

Nonetheless, as London reported, most of these people preferred to maintain this life so long as their health would allow rather than go to the workhouse, where the severity of the conditions was designed to instruct that vagrancy was next to Godlessness. Many Edwardians firmly believed that if there were idle rich at one end of the social scale there were certainly idle poor at the other, who probably had only themselves to blame for their idleness.

There were other Edwardians who were not content to turn their backs on the problems of the cities, but sought instead new ways of resolving them. One of these new ideas was town planning, a term first devised in the middle of the Edwardian age and developed from the concept of the 'garden city'. The garden city was the idea of Ebenezer Howard, first put forward in his book *Tomorrow*, published in 1898, and re-issued in 1902 as *Garden Cities of Tomorrow*. The Victorians had built several paternalistic company towns during the last decades of the

nineteenth century, the most notable of which were the Cadbury family's Bournville, near Birmingham, and the Lever Brothers' Port Sunlight, in the Wirral. Howard's plan was to build cities in open country which would combine an urban community with the rural advantages of light and health, and which would not be dependent on the benevolence of one company but would stand as a Trust owning the freehold of an area in which industry would be operated by communities of some 30,000 people, and which would be surrounded by carefully but intensively farmed green belts.

The first garden city was started in 1903 at Letchworth in Hertfordshire, and by 1914 some 9,000 people were living and working as a balanced community where only 400 had lived before. In spite of this success no attempts were made during the Edwardian period to copy it elsewhere, though the concept was adapted for the planned extension of existing towns, rather than the creation of entirely new ones, as with the Hampstead Garden Suburb, started in 1907. Such projects were the start of overall

The Caledonian Market in 1912, where on Fridays bargain-hunters gathered in search of everything from old masters and rare plate to rusty bolts and chipped china. On Mondays and Thursdays the area was used as London's cattle-market. Drawing by Cyrus Cuneo.

urban planning, as opposed to the piecemeal approach adopted by the Victorians, and the Liberal Government of 1909 gave official blessing to the concept with its Housing and Town Planning Act, which the President of the Local Government Board claimed would secure 'the home healthy, the house beautiful, the town pleasant, the city dignified, and the suburb salubrious.' The Act failed to live up to such promises. It did not concern itself with existing towns, and it did not produce the additional houses that were needed to meet the increase in population. The result was that overcrowding got worse rather than better in the later Edwardian years, and the plans of some of the era's more enlightened men for improving the nation's cities were not, and have never since been, accomplished.

Railways remained supreme for long-distance travel in Britain, and railway traffic increased every year during the Edwardian age. Top, inauguration of the new Great Western Railway express service from Penzance to London in July, 1901. Above, the Brighton Railway Company opened Victoria Station in 1908. Right, interior of the Pullman cars introduced by the London, Brighton and South Coast Railway in 1906. Facing page, the Edwardian system of arranging railway timetables by stretching threads to represent each train's journey.

"The motor-omnibus", reported *The Illustrated London News* in 1905, "has come to stay", the bus having the same attraction "for the masses" as the motor car "for the classes". Top, a Vanguard bus carefully photographed before starting on its daily run to Brighton and back. The Argyll car introduced in 1908, was designed especially for doctors. The 1905 motor show, top right, shows some of the cars designed for distinguished people, including, in the foreground, a Daimler built for picnic excursions by the Princess of Wales.

The ambulance, right, was patented in 1909. The new London motor bus which, even in 1903 when it was quite rare, was recognised as a rival to the electric tram. By 1913 there were some 3,000 buses on the streets of London and the position of the tram was rapidly being undermined. Far right, a wrecked car after collision with a tram. In Edwardian times such accidents made news.

"Fair motorists examining an engine" ran the caption to the illustration from the 1908 motor show, above. *The Illustrated London News* noted that woman had long passed the stage where she was content to be a mere passenger: "she is now a skilled driver and very often something of a mechanic". Right, C. S. Rolls, joint founder of the motor car manufacturers, photographed in his 80 horse-power racing car in 1903.

Top, going to the races — a contrast in styles of transport to Ascot in 1906.

Above, an electric fire-engine built for the London Fire Brigade in 1911. The accumulators for storing the electric power were housed beneath the bonnet.

Right, the $3\frac{1}{2}$ horse-power Humber motor cycle and side-car, photographed beside the Forth Bridge in 1912.

The rapid growth in the number and improved performance of motor cars had disastrous effects on untarred roads,

and in spite of insistent public demand it was some years before main roads were macadamized.

3 COUNTRY LIFE

The countryside was in a sad state of decay when Edward ascended the throne. Agriculture, the oldest and for so long the largest industry in Britain, had lost its dominance. The technological innovations in farming, such as mechanical harvesters and multi-furrow ploughs, had been adopted in the United States of America and other overseas countries long before they were in this country (though the first petrol-driven tractor was produced here in 1902 by Dan Albone, of Biggleswade), and this enabled their products, carried swiftly by the newly developed network of railways and steamship services, to undercut those of the British farmers. The result was that the acreage of land under cultivation fell substantially; between 1870 and 1914 the national corn area declined by 30 per cent, and when the First World War broke out Britain was having to import one half of all food consumed. At the same time agricultural employment was declining. At the start of the reign 77 per cent of the population was resident in urban districts, and this trend continued during the early years of the new century. It was not just arable farming that suffered from foreign competition. Refrigerated meat was now being brought in from Argentina and New Zealand, and dairy products such as bacon, butter and cheese from Denmark and the Netherlands. The decline of the rural areas of England was not a new phenomenon: it dated back to enclosures, which deprived agricultural labourers of the common land on which they grazed cows, cut turf for fuel, and kept their geese and hens. The introduction of enclosures was succinctly criticised by the verse of the time:

'The law locks up the man or woman,
Who steals the goose from off the common;
But lets the greater villain loose,
Who steals the common off the goose!

In the end the English farmers who did best in Edwardian times were those who adapted themselves to providing for the immediate demands of the nearest town, either by market gardening, or growing fruit, or producing milk. Dairying was beginning to develop into an industry, helped by mechanisation; the cream separator was well established in Edwardian times, and milking machines had been invented, but farmers were slow to adopt them. More important was the improvement of communications, for railways could carry milk churns into the cities in time to reach the businessman's breakfast table, and the development of the motor lorry brought more and more farmers within reach of railway stations. And milk was becoming safe to drink, though pasteurisation was not yet compulsory. There was a gradual but substantial increase in the cattle population during Edwardian times, and the area of permanent grassland almost doubled between 1870 and 1914.

The arrest of the retreat from the land towards the end of Edward's reign was partly due to the growth of the dairy industry and partly to the Smallholdings Act of 1907, which was designed to push local authorities into greater activity in the creation of holdings for small farmers. In the seven years before 1914 some 14,000 new holdings, covering about 200,000 acres, were set up. By the end of the reign the number of agricultural workers had stabilised at around 750,000, while the total of those engaged in agriculture, including market gardeners, was about 1,250,000. Nonetheless the contribution of agriculture to the national product continued to fall, and for the Edwardian period as a whole averaged not much more than 6 per cent.

In such circumstances it was inevitable that the countryside appealed mainly to lovers of nature and the poets of solitude. Few stayed who could find employment elsewhere, and C. F. G. Masterman, in *The Condition of England* (1909), noted that the villages of England were being increasingly left to old women and children, while the ancient skilled occupations were becoming lost arts. A clergyman in Somerset recalled that his village had no social life at all: 'A village which once fed, clothed, policed and regulated itself cannot now dig its own wells or build its own barns. Still less can it act its own dramas, build its own church, or organise its own work and play. It is pathetically helpless in everything . . . England is bleeding at the arteries, and it is her reddest blood which is flowing away.' Those who did continue to live in the country were more concerned about obtaining running water, electric light and reliable drainage than they were about preserving picturesque cottages or the customs of the past. Villages gradually developed into satellites of the town where, for example, a wider variety of goods could be obtained than from the village store. Flora Thompson, in *Lark Rise to Candleford* (1945), described the changing village: 'Candleford Green was at that time a separate village. In a few years it was to become part of Candleford. Already the rows of villas were stretching out towards it; but as yet the green with its spreading oak, with the white-painted seats, its roofed-in well with the chained bucket, its church spire soaring out of trees, and its cluster of old cottages, was untouched by change.' But change was coming, for she records how within a few years the local carpenter, his son and grandson vanished from

The King, having taken several prizes for his Southdowns, inspected the sheep with particular attention during a visit to the Royal Agricultural Society's Show at Derby in 1906.

the village, two of them dying within a year of each other in the village, the third being killed in the Boer War. Their shop was demolished 'to make way for a builder's showroom with baths and tiled fireplaces and W.C. pans in the window.

Country trades found it increasingly difficult to survive the competition of the better organised and more economical sources of supply that were infiltrating the villages from outside, aided of course by the improvements in communications. The rural housewife found a far greater choice of goods, including clothes and furnishings offered on instalment systems, brought to her door, as well as groceries. She may well not have had to bake her own bread, because the baker would call; so too would the butcher, with imported frozen meat cheaper than the local fresh meat would be, and the grocer with tins and packaged foods — a lazy extravagance, in the view of some contemporary commentators, and one in which not many could afford to indulge. In mid-Edwardian times the average weekly earnings of rural labourers was 17s 6d, which was well below Seebohm Rowntree's poverty line for a family of any size. In the village of Corsley, in Wiltshire, about a third of all the families were living below the poverty line, according to an investigation carried out by Miss Maud F. Davies, and published in *Life in an English Village* in 1909. Miss Davies reported on the situation of a labourer with wife and five children. He earned 15s a week, paid 1s 6d a week rent for his cottage, 5s a year for an allotment and 2s 5d a month to a Friendly Society. During one week in January, 1906, the family bought the following:

½lb tea, 8d. 3lb sugar, 5½d. 1½lb butter, 1s 6d. Bacon, 1s 4d. Quaker oats, 5½d. 2oz tobacco, 6d. Cheese, 9d. ½lb lard, 2½d. ¼lb suet, 2d. Baking powder, 1d. Papers, 2d. 1lb soap, 3d. Oranges, 2d. ½lb currants, 1½d. 1 pint beer, 2d. Coal, 1s 2½d. Loaf, 2¼d. Milk, 6½d. Butter, 4d. Sugar, 2¼d. Loaf, 2¼d. Oil, 2½d. Stockings, 6½d. Bread bill, 3s. Total, 13s 4¾d.

Provision of allotments was one of the ways the Government tried to help the rural poor, and the 5s a year this man paid in rent for an allotment would have been money well spent, for it should have provided his family with the fresh vegetables they clearly needed. But it was noted that many of the new allotments created by the various Allotment Acts of the time went not to labourers but to tradesmen, many councils having made it a rule not to provide them for applicants with less capital than £10 an acre. Farmers were often far from keen on their labourers renting allotments, which might absorb energy that would otherwise be devoted to farm work,

Above, an oil-powered tractor, vintage 1911, demonstrating its prowess in crossing a ditch.

Right, the Lawrence-Kennedy cow milker, designed to be powered by electricity, oil, gas, steam or water, and a new hand-milking machine – both dating from 1904. Farmers were not enthusiastic about milking machines.

and some of those labourers that acquired them soon gave them up in despair because of the havoc wreaked by the protected game bred on the local estates. The other opportunity a labourer would take if he could to supplement his family's meagre fare was to keep a pig, every part of which would be turned to use when it was slaughtered in the autumn. Villagers often set up pig clubs to help one another buy a piglet and insure it against too early or untimely a death.

The traditions of the agricultural community, with its well-ordered relationship between manor and village, landowner and tenant, farmer and labourer, were long established and slow to change, though the Edwardian era brought developments which were more significant than was perhaps recognised at the time. The series of Agricultural Holding Acts gave tenants much greater security, allowed them to farm as they liked rather than at the dictate of the landowners, and even awarded them compensation for damage caused to crops by game birds which they were not entitled to shoot. Change was also coming, though far more slowly than in industrial England, in the relationship between a labourer and his employer. In July, 1906, George Edwards launched the Eastern Counties Agricultural Labourers' and Smallholders' Union in North Walsham, Norfolk, and within a year forty-nine branches had been opened in East Anglia. The first

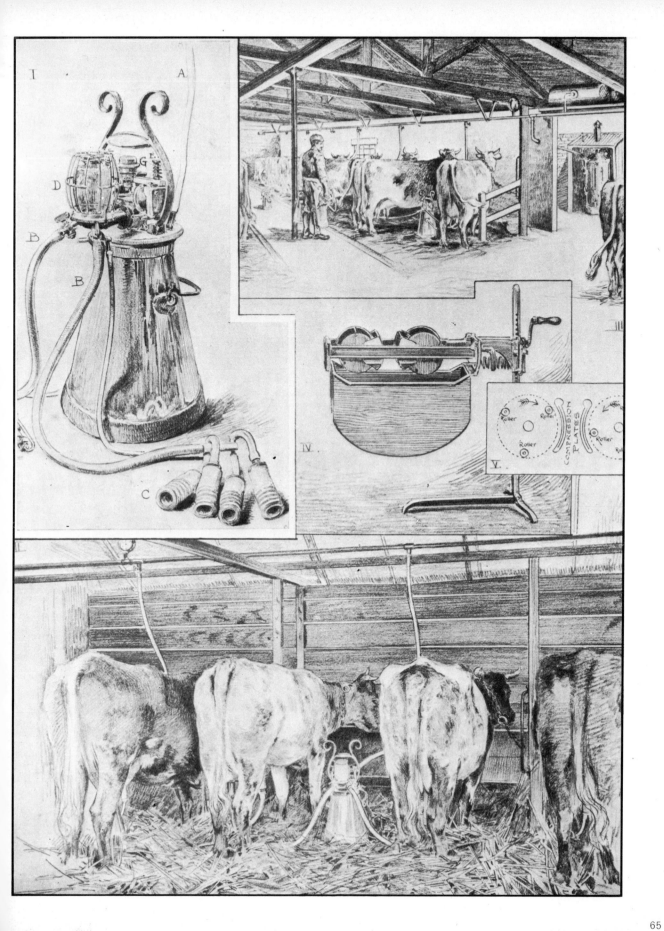

Above, up-to-date agriculture, 1905. The first petrol-driven tractor was produced at Biggleswade three years earlier, but farmers in this country were slow to develop it compared with their competitors in other countries. Right, August lavender-picking at Mitcham in Surrey, whose fields in the early 1900s rivalled those of France.

organised strike took place three years later, but the farmers were not prepared to meet the union to discuss their disputes. It was the State, rather than the traditional village leader, the squire, that came in to help, and thus to begin to break up the old order. For many villagers much the most significant step was the introduction, in 1908, of the Old Age Pensions Act, which had the effect of transforming life for the aged cottagers of Candleford, as Flora Thomson described: 'They were relieved of anxiety. They were suddenly rich. Independent for life! At first when they went to the Post Office to draw it, tears of gratitude would run down the cheeks of some, and they would say as they picked up their money, "God bless that Lloyd George . . . and God bless you, miss!", and there were flowers from their gardens and apples from their trees for the girl who merely handed them the money.'

Outside the village, and at the other end of the social and economic scale, lay the source of perhaps the greatest displays of private ostentation in Edwardian times — the country house. The countryside was dominated by these houses, as it has not been since, and the long weekend parties given in them have been the subject of so much literary description, in fact and fiction, that they have become, along with the King himself, the best-known and most nostalgic feature of the age, indelibly associated with the summer of 1911, whose record temperatures brought out the

sunshades and boaters which are better remembered today than the damaging floods brought by so many Edwardian winters. The Edwardian weekend was described by Sir Harold Nicolson in *Small Talk* (1937) as 'the most agreeable form of social intercourse that the world has ever known', and he described some of its features:

'People were called by their valets at eight-thirty. These silent but hostile men would arrive bearing in their left hand a neat brass can of shaving water, and in their right hand a neat brass tray of tea, toast, and Marie biscuits. The Edwardian, blinking plethoric eyes above his pink silk eiderdown, would munch the biscuits and sip the tea. He would then adjust his teeth, adjust his hair, adjust his Afghan dressing-robe, and slouch plethoric along the passage to the bathroom . . .'

Having completed his toilet, he descended 'down the red pile staircases', to breakfast:

'Only the really improper Edwardians had breakfast in their room. The others met, on that Sunday morning, in the dining-room. The smell of last night's port

had given place to the smell of this morning's spirit of wine. Rows of little spirit lamps warmed rows of large silver dishes. On a table to the right between the windows were grouped Hams, Tongues, Galantines, Cold Grouse, ditto Pheasant, ditto Partridge, ditto Ptarmigan. No Edwardian meal was complete without Ptarmigan. Hot or cold . . . On a further table, to the left between the doors, stood fruits of different calibre, and jugs of cold water, and jugs of lemonade. A fourth table contained porridge utensils. A fifth coffee, and pots of Indian and China tea. The latter were differentiated from each other by little ribbons of yellow (indicating China) and red (indicating, without *arrière pensée*, our Indian Empire). The centre table, which was prepared for twenty-three people, would be bright with Malmaisons and toast-racks. No newspapers were, at this stage, allowed.

'The atmosphere of the Edwardian dining-room at nine-thirty was essentially daring. A pleasant sense of confederacy and sin hung above the smell of the spirit-lamps. For had they not all been brought up to attend family prayers? And had they not all eluded that obligation? It was true, of course, that the host and hostess, with their niece, had at nine proceeded to the family chapel and heard the butler reading a short collect for the day. But the guests had for their part evaded these Victorian obligations. The corporate evasion gave to the proceedings an atmosphere of dash. There was no insincerity in the bright gaiety with which they greeted each other, with which they discussed how he or she had slept. "A little kedgeree, Lady Maude?" "Oh, thank you Mr Stapleton." Evidently it was all going very well.'

And so on, through a morning at church, luncheon, an afternoon drive in an open Daimler, tea served in the blue gallery, bridge, dinner ('Ptarmigan and champagne'), bridge again, and finally at midnight, devilled chicken in the Holbein room. Then, next morning:

'Their valets would pack their Enos and their shooting-sticks. They would return by train to London. Their carriages would meet them, horses champing bits, at the arrival platform of Paddington. In the train coming up the members of the house-party would read in the *Morning Post* a list of the members of the house-party. They returned to Curzon Street feeling very pleased indeed. And next Saturday it would all begin again.'

Country house parties were used on occasions for serious purposes, though not always with serious results. Julian Amery, in his biography of Joseph Chamberlain, described what happened at Chatsworth when, under cover of a house party assembled for amateur theatricals, Baron von Eckardstein was in-

Top, The Country Girl: one of a series of "Peculiarly British Types" published in 1911.

Centre, a weekend cottage for £200. The builders offered to help their clients find suitable sites in any part of the kingdom.

Right, the development of market gardening was one of British agriculture's responses to the growing dominance of foreign arable and dairy products during the Edwardian era. One farm adopting French methods was that of Thatcham, near Newbury.

INTENSIVE CULTIVATION

A pictorial lesson in the French methods, now widely used in Great Britain, by which a great impulse has been given to market gardening in this country.

A TIME-SAVING CAN

The watering cans employed in the French system have enormous "roses," which enable the watering to be carried out with great despatch.

PACKING PRODUCE FOR THE MARKET

The question of packing and sending to market is one of the many elements upon which the working of the scheme depends, and both at the Thatcham Farm, which forms the subject of our illustrations, and elsewhere, our market gardeners are gradually adopting the methods which have proved so successful in France.

A SHOWER IN A SECOND

The cans are emptied over the produce in second or two—an important point in a process in which every moment of time is of value.

COVERING PLANTS WITH MATTING

Mats are extensively used, being placed over the frames to shield fresh plants from too much sun in the heat of summer, and for protection against frost during the winter and early spring.

PLANTS IN THEIR FRAMES

The seed, specially imported from France, is found to yield best in these frames. The beds are dug spade deep, and carefully manured.

THE "CLOCHES" OR BELL-GLASSES

These glass domes are used to protect the crops in the early part of the year, one thousand being required for an acre of ground. The illustration shows a number of cloches stored for the summer months.

vited to meet Chamberlain to discuss Anglo-German relations: 'Among the guests at Chatsworth were two young people much in love. On the very night of the Baron's talk with Chamberlain they arranged to meet in *her* room when the company was retired. But Chatsworth, as Dr Johnson once remarked, is "a very fine house", and the young man, fearing to mistake another room for his lady's, asked her to leave a sign to show which was her door. On the spur of the moment she promised to drop a large sandwich on the floor outside. Now Eckardstein was a voracious eater, accustomed to devour a whole cold chicken before retiring. That evening, however, the prolonged discussion of foreign affairs had intercepted his hopes of lighter refreshment. Hungry and morose he was retiring to bed when, as he walked along the passage to his room, he saw a sandwich lying on the floor. Making sure he was alone, he pounced upon his dusty prey. In an instant it was devoured; and the course of true love was made less smooth than ever.'

A little night movement between the bedrooms of these rambling country houses was not unusual, though Edwardian determination to keep up appearances ensured that it was carried out with the utmost discretion. Victoria Sackville-West, in her novel *The Edwardians*, described how the Edwardian hostess might set about arranging things for the convenience of her guests:

'The name of each guest would be neatly written on a card slipped into a tiny brass frame on the bedroom door. This question of the disposition of bedrooms always gave the duchess and her fellow-hostesses cause for anxious thought. It was so necessary to be tactful, and at the same time discreet. The professional Lothario would be furious if he found himself in a room surrounded by ladies who were all accompanied by their husbands. Tommy Brand, on such occasions, had been known to leave the house on a Sunday morning — thank goodness, thought the duchess, that wasn't at Chevron! Romola Cheyne, who always neatly sized up everybody in a phrase — very illuminating and convenient — said that Tommy's motto was "*Chacun a sa Chacune*". Then there were the recognised lovers to be considered; the duchess herself would have been annoyed had she gone to stay at the same party as Harry Tremaine, only to find that he had been put at the other end of the house. (But she was getting tired of Harry Tremaine.) It was part of a good hostess' duty to see to such things; they must be made easy, though not too obvious. So she always planned the rooms carefully with Miss Wace, occasionally wondering whether that upright and virtuous virgin was ever struck by the recurrence of certain adjustments and coincidences . . .'

Above, informal picnic at the meet of the Devon and Somerset staghounds. Reproduced in 1908 from the painting by J. W. Hammick.

Right, the Grand Hotel, Llandudno, was opened in 1902 to enhance the attractions of "the Queen of Welsh watering-places".

All this fevered weekend activity was made possible, of course, by the development of the railways and more especially by the advent of the motor car. But not everyone in the country welcomed the idea that the motor car would, as *The Illustrated London News* had suggested in 1903, make the whole world kin. The paper published, on May 9, the response of one Edwardian misanthrope to this suggestion:

'Sir, this is no satisfaction to me. I have spent my life in escaping from my kindred. A year or two ago I took a house in the country, six miles from a railway station, and a hundred miles from my nearest relations, who when they are moved by family affection to visit me, have to make a tiresome journey in at least

three trains. They have not made the journey yet. But yesterday I received a letter from them, stating that they proposed to buy a motor car, which would then bring them over to my place to lunch, and take them back in time for dinner (unless I, with my usual generosity, asked them to stay the night), and all for a shilling's worth of petrol.'

Probably the most eloquent contemporary critic of Edwardian life as typified by the country house was the journalist and Liberal politician, C. F. G. Masterman, who recognised that the speeding up of living had brought a great increase of waste, and that the standard of life had been raised not so much in comfort as in ostentation. 'Where one house sufficed now two are demanded; where a dinner of a certain quality, now a dinner of a superior quality; where clothes or dresses or flowers, now more clothes, more dresses, more flowers. It is waste, not because fine clothes and rare flowers and pleasant food are in themselves undesirable, but because by a kind of parallel of the law of diminishing returns in agriculture, additional expenditure in such directions fails to result in correspondent additions of happiness . . .

Edwardians carried on the Victorian enthusiasm for holidays by the sea.
Top, first photograph of the new marine drive in Scarborough, shortly before its opening on July 27, 1908. Above, the bathing-hour at a south coast seaside resort.

Right, the first garden city was started in 1903 at Letchworth, in Hertfordshire, and the houses illustrated here were designed for that area as an attractive but cheap answer to the jerry building which, *The Illustrated London News* reported in 1905, had turned the outskirts of London into "an abomination of desolation".

'Public penury, private ostentation — that, perhaps, is the heart of the complaint. A nation with the wealth of England can afford to spend, and spend royally. Only the end should be itself desirable, and the choice deliberate. The spectacle of a huge urban poverty confronts all this waste energy. That spectacle should not, indeed, forbid all luxuries and splendours; but it should condemn the less rewarding of them as things tawdry and mean.'

Cottage costing £150
Walls. exterior brick nogging
internal 6 in stud partitions
Harry Prince Esq

2 Bedrooms
living room &
scullery

Cottage costing £148
Hollow concrete
blocks
Cement Products
Company

Living room
Kitchen
Scullery
Bathroom
Hall
3 Bedrooms

Cottage costing £150
Timber framed walls
on concrete foundations
Lionel F
Crane Esq

Living room
scullery with bath
2 Bedrooms

Living room
Scullery
3 Bedrooms

Living room, Scullery,
3 Bedrooms

£150 Cottage of Concrete
Monolithic Walls
(Potter & Company Ld)

Walls 9in brick

3 Cottages
cost £525 or £175 each
Ivor Tucker Esq

Cottage costing £140.
Charles
Gustave
Agate Esq

Brick walls
Outside rough cast

Cottage Costing £165
W. Gladwell & Co. Ld.

Pair of Cottages. cost £420
Brick. rough cast
(Baillie Scott Esq)

In each. Kitchen living room
Parlour
Scullery
3 Bedrooms

In each. Living room
Kitchen-Scullery
3 Bedrooms. Landing for
clothes chest.
Larder
coals.
bath etc.

Roof Mansard
Tiled.
Could be
erected in
five weeks

Semi detached cottages Costing £128 each
Walls 9in asbestic brick
V. Dunkerley

A Hugh Fisher

Cottage Costing £150. Brick covered with Portland Cement

4 WORK

Compared with what was to follow, the Edwardian years were peaceful and prosperous. Though the prosperity was unevenly shared and the domestic peace was disturbed by the Irish rebellion, labour disputes and the increasing militancy of the campaign for women's suffrage, these only ruffled the surface of the general aura of well-being that characterised the first decade of the twentieth century. In strictly economic terms there is no doubting that the Edwardians did well. The value of the country's exports rose from £304 million in 1900 to £635 million in 1913. Exports grew more rapidly than imports — about one third of the products of industry went overseas — and there was a modest trade surplus. In addition the rapid increase in British capital holdings abroad was yielding returns of nearly £200 million a year by 1913. At the same time Britain was visibly declining from that peak of world economic dominance that she had achieved in 1870s. By the time Edward succeeded to the throne Britain had been overtaken in the output of coal and iron by the United States, and in steel by both the United States and Germany. These two countries were challenging Britain's position as the world's largest exporter of manufactured goods, and that they were challenging from increasing strength was revealed by the statistics showing comparative growth rates for the years 1870 to the outbreak of the First World War, which showed that the British rate had been 2·2 per cent whereas in America the rate had been 4·3 per cent and in Germany 2·9 per cent.

This competition did not go unnoticed, and was the frequent subject of comment in the Edwardian press, pamphlets, books and political speeches. It was also the inspiration for the determined attack upon free trade that was carried on, ultimately without success, by the tariff reformers led by Joseph Chamberlain. It was noted that much of the new machinery used by British industry was being made in America and Germany, though one of the major criticisms of industry at this time was that not enough new machinery was being used, for perhaps too much investment was going abroad. *The Times* noted in 1912 that there were far too many obsolete engineering works in the country, using old Victorian machinery and old Victorian working methods. 'Such people often complain about unfair competition', said *The Times*, 'but if any suggestion is made to them about improvements they excuse themselves in busy times by saying that they cannot afford to stop any part of their works for alterations, and in slack times they say

Above, casting six-inch shells for naval guns at the Royal Arsenal, Woolwich.

Right, in 1903 work began to electrify the District Railway. Piles were driven into the canal-bed at Lot's Road, Chelsea, on which the power station was then built.

they have no money to spend on new ideas.' A study of comparative industrial efficiency in England, America and Germany, published in 1919, suggested that the sons and grandsons of enterprising Victorians in this country had too many other interests. 'The once enterprising manufacturer has grown slack', it concluded. 'He has let the business take care of itself, while he is shooting grouse or yachting in the Mediterranean. That is *his* business. The once unequalled workman has adopted the motto: "Get as much and do as little as possible"; *his* business is football or betting. Each blames the other.'

Of all British industries, coal was the greatest contributor to the country's prosperity. Output and employment rose steadily, reaching a peak of 287 million tons in 1913. The balance of activity continued to go to the more recently developed mining areas of Yorkshire, Wales and the East

Midlands, but the demand for coal, stimulated by export markets, was such that even the older areas of Northumberland, Lancashire and the Black Country were kept busy. Coal miners were among the better paid workers in Edwardian times, and some of their conditions of work were greatly improved. Under the Mines (Eight Hours) Act of 1908 their working hours were controlled by the first statutory regulation brought in to limit the hours of work for adult males, as distinct from women and children. In 1912 the Coal Mines (Minimum Wage) Act laid down a minimum wage structure for the industry, and miners also benefited from the other social legislation brought in by the Liberal Government of 1906. Improved wages and benefits, however, were not accompanied by greater productivity; indeed the output per miner fell from 290 tons a year to less than 260 tons after 1910. This was partly due to the arduous conditions in which miners still had to work, and partly to the failure of the pit owners to install new machinery, such as cutters and conveyors, that was now available.

Other traditional British industries did even less well. Agriculture, as was seen in the previous chapter, was in the doldrums for much of the time. The textile industries had failed to install badly needed new equipment towards the end of the nineteenth century, and by 1901 both the cotton and the woollen industries reported declines in employment. But as the twentieth century advanced so both industries began to recover, though expansion and prosperity still did not persuade mill-owners to replace old equipment; it was reported that in Britain in 1913, for example, the cotton mule outnumbered the newer ring spindle by four to one, whereas in the United States the proportion was eight to one in favour of ring spindles which were far more productive. And though cotton exports boomed (in 1901 Britain exported 5,365 million yards of piece goods, in 1913 the figure had risen to 7,075) they were taking advantage of the less competitive markets in the Empire.

Iron and steel manufacture also relied heavily on the Empire for its exports, and was failing to respond effectively to foreign competition. British steel production increased by one fifth between 1900 and 1910, whereas that of the United States rose by 150 per cent and Germany's by 100 per cent. However, as Professor Arthur J. Taylor has pointed out in his essay on the Edwardian economy in *Edwardian England*, the shortcomings of the primary industry could be readily forgotten in the achievements of the engineer. 'By 1911 the mechanical and electrical engineering industries, in their various branches, were employing two and a half times as many men as iron and steel; and it was in these industries, growing rapidly even

Above, the King and Queen visit the Vickers steel works at Sheffield in 1905.

Top right, the opening by the King of the No 9 Dock on the Manchester Ship Canal, in July 1905.

Right, advertisement published in *The Illustrated London News* of 1907, and designed to take advantage of the public enthusiasm for the new transatlantic liner that went into service that year and recaptured the blue riband for the fastest crossing.

in the years of the Great Depression, that the forward thrust of Edwardian economic expansion was most heavily concentrated.' The most significant engineering activities were in the making of power-engines and industrial machinery and in ship and railway building. Britain's continuing pre-eminence in shipbuilding was reflected in the fact that in 1914, in spite of intense

THE "MAURETANIA" AND COLMAN'S D.S.F. MUSTARD

How perfect everything is here!
I see the mustard is Colman's.

Colman's Mustard follows the flag and
maintains the record for British reliability
and perfection.   *Accept no substitute.*

foreign competition, three-fifths of the world's ships were being built in British yards. They included some of the largest transatlantic liners, such as the *Mauretania* (which came into service in 1907, and recaptured from Germany the blue riband for the fastest crossing) and the ill-fated 46,328 tons *Titanic*, which was launched in May, 1911, from the yards of Harland & Wolff in Belfast, and sank on her maiden voyage in the early morning of April 15, 1912, after hitting an iceberg, with the loss of some 1,500 lives. It was an appalling disaster, but 706 of the passengers and crew were saved after the liner's SOS wireless messages were picked up by the Cunard liner *Carpathia*, which steamed 58 miles to the rescue and, though the *Titanic* had disappeared, found some of its lifeboats scattered over the area. It was in 1901 that Marconi had first sent messages from Cornwall, in England, across the Atlantic to Newfoundland, to demonstrate the invention of wireless telegraphy, and the *Titanic* disaster was dramatic evidence of its value.

Another development that may fairly be credited to Edwardian times was that of powered flight, though not much of the early credit could be claimed by the British. The first successful flights by Wilbur and Orville Wright in North Carolina in 1903 caused less of a stir in Britain than did the first flight across the Channel, achieved, unhappily for Edwardian pride, by the Frenchman Bleriot on July 25, 1909. The *Daily*

In 1912 the vast 46,328-ton liner *Titanic* sank after hitting an iceberg on her maiden voyage. Some 1,500 of those on

board lost their lives, but 706 were saved.

Above left, Poldhu Station, in Cornwall, from which Marconi, above right, sent and received his first wireless messages to and from Newfoundland in December, 1901. Right, the "D1", then the largest submarine in the world, was fitted out in 1910 so that it could receive wireless messages even when submerged.

Mail offered £10,000 for the first flight between London and Manchester, and this was accomplished in 1910. Of more immediate significance to Edwardians was the transition from the horse-drawn to mechanically propelled vehicles, which was achieved by way of the bicycle. Flora Thompson described the early days of cycling when the new low safety-bicycle had superseded the penny-farthing. In those days cycling clubs would send telegrams home from their farthest point, either to report their safe arrival or to prove how far they had actually travelled, 'for a cyclist's word as to his day's mileage then ranked with an angler's account of his catch.' Before long every man, youth and boy in Candleford whose finances were above the poverty line was riding a bicycle, and though men tried to keep the privilege of riding to their own sex it was to no avail. The wife of a doctor in the district was the first woman to be seen on a bicycle there. 'I should like to tear her off that thing and smack her pretty little backside', growled one man in the village. But one woman after another 'appeared riding a glittering new bicycle. In long skirts, it is true, but with most of their petticoats left in the bedroom behind them.'

In November 1905 more than 7,000 unemployed marched from the East End of London into Hyde Park to demand work and condemn the dole.

674·1892
A Mechanical Contrivance
for fishing with rod and line.

19769'98
Pneumatic Boat
for Sportsmen.

5024'85
Section of a
Walking Sh
with W

25838'95
See-saw Motion
utilized for
Propelling
vessels

1364·1783 (Early Patent)
A Machine for use as a Fire
Escape and "to gather fruit
from trees"

10452'88
Umbrella with a Gutter

8229'85
An Umbrella
with holes for
ventilation.
The openings
are protected by a
second smaller umbrella

SECTION

24701'96
A Boat driven by
Wind-mills.

1959'97
A Padded Chair and
Revolving Carrier attached to
Car to prevent serious accidents.

4917'91   SECTION
Holder for Cigars or small
articles for use within a Hat.

2606'88
A Sunshade.

1009'80
An Umbrella Cap

6569'94   A Perambulator with detacha
wheels   The body folds up
and forms a hand bag.

Edwardians were not lacking in invention, as was shown by these imaginative ideas from the Patent Office records of

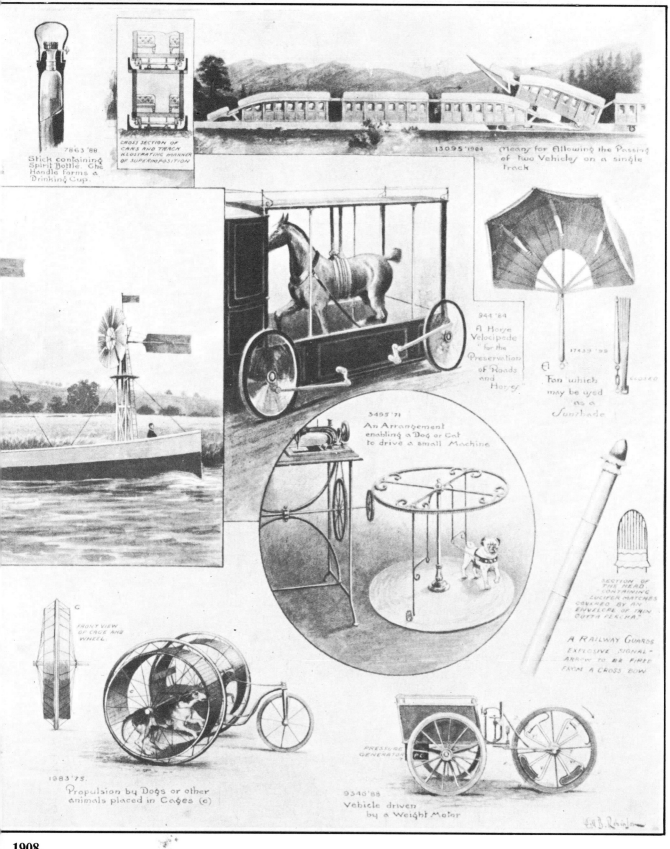

7863 '88
Stick containing
Spirit Bottle. The
Handle forms a
Drinking Cup.

CROSS SECTION OF
CARS AND TRACK
ILLUSTRATING MANNER
OF SUPERIMPOSITION

13095 1904   Means for Allowing the Passing
of two Vehicles on a single
Track

944 '84
A Horse
Velocipede
"for the
Preservation
of Roads
and
Horses"

17459 '99
A Fan which
may be used
as a
Sunshade   CLOSED

3495 '71
An Arrangement
enabling a Dog or Cat
to drive a small Machine

FRONT VIEW
OF CAGE AND
WHEEL.

SECTION OF
THE HEAD
CONTAINING
LUCIFER MATCHES
COVERED BY AN
ENVELOPE OF THIN
GUTTA PERCHA.

A RAILWAY GUARDS
EXPLOSIVE SIGNAL-
ARROW TO BE FIRED
FROM A CROSS BOW

1083 '75.
Propulsion by Dogs or other
animals placed in Cages (c)

PRESSURE
GENERATOR

9540 '88
Vehicle driven
by a Weight Motor

1908.

At the turn of the century it seemed that everyone under forty was awheel. Though the origins of the car, which developed from the flourishing pedal cycle business, clearly lay in Victorian times, it was during Edward's reign that the motor car ceased to be an adventure and became a convenience. The King was an early enthusiast, and he helped overcome popular ignorance by giving his patronage to the Automobile Club of Great Britain and Ireland, which thus became the Royal Automobile Club. In 1905 the RAC started the Tourist Trophy event in the Isle of Man, won that year by John S. Napier at an average speed of 33·9 mph, and in the following year by C. S. Rolls, who had already entered into partnership with Henry Royce to manufacture cars. Within two years the first Rolls-Royce six-cylinder Silver Ghost had been produced. Registration of vehicles became compulsory in 1903, when 23,000 were registered and when the speed limit was raised from 14 mph to 20. By 1910 the number had risen to over 100,000. As an industry the manufacture of motor cars grew fast, but until the outbreak of war Britain was an importer rather than an exporter of cars, the United States having gained a long lead. Henry Ford had established his first assembly line for mass-produced cars in Detroit in 1903, and by 1914, when the total number of private cars in Britain was 132,000, some 20,000 Ford cars had been assembled in this country. *The Times*, in 1912, had warned that a valuable market would be lost if a British manufacturer did not 'set himself seriously to work to produce small cars as good and as cheap as those now imported from abroad.' In the same year William Morris, later Lord Nuffield, revealed that the Morris Oxford car was about to go into mass production, though it had only just done so when war broke out.

Aeroplanes and motor cars, electric underground trains and escalators, telephones, typewriters, wireless and gramophones — the Edwardian age saw the development and acceptance into common use of many of the trappings (we would now call them essentials) of the twentieth century. Of equally fundamental significance to the majority of Edwardians, and to all Britons since, was the burst of social reform that followed the Liberal Party's victory in the general election of 1906, legislation which was the origin of the welfare state in Britain. Sir Henry Campbell-Bannerman, the Liberal leader, had promised when

Right, a proposal to dam the Thames by building a barrage at Gravesend, with four locks for the passage of shipping and a railway tunnel beneath, was put forward in January, 1905, as an answer to the Port of London Authority's continuing problem of the river's tidal flow.

The new railway bridge over the River Tyne at Newcastle was opened by the King on July 10, 1906, when the royal train stopped on the middle of the bridge.

An extension of the Devonport dockyard, at Plymouth, including a dry dock 650 feet long to take the latest naval warships, was completed in 1907.

Top, the Port of London in 1908, when Lloyd George put forward his plans to purchase the docks for the State. Above, scene at the Albert Dock when the unclaimed effects of men who had died or been lost at sea were sold by auction.

Right, an explosion at Maypole Colliery at Abram, near Wigan, caused the loss of 70 lives in August, 1908. Coal was the greatest contributor to Edwardian prosperity, both output and employment rising steadily throughout this period.

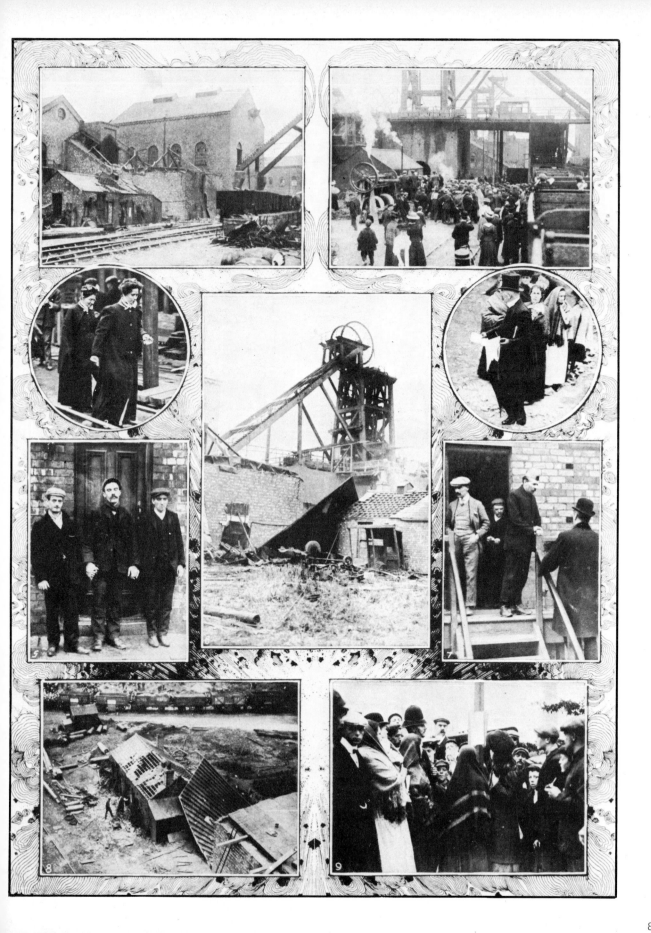

his party came to power that England would become 'less of a pleasure ground for the rich and more of a treasure house for the nation', and his Government began by introducing the Trades Disputes Act which gave the trade unions the protection for their funds which had been removed by the Taff Vale judgment of 1901. In 1908 the Old Age Pensions Act provided old people over 70 with 5s a week (7s 6d for married couples) 'as of right', though it was tied to a means test. In 1909 the Trade Boards Act established boards with powers to fix minimum wages for workers in some 'sweated labour' industries, and in the same year Labour Exchanges were set up to help the unemployed find jobs in their area. In 1911 a contributory insurance scheme was introduced for the payment of sickness and unemployment benefits. A note written by Lloyd George, who introduced the scheme, and dated March 7, 1911, set out the way it was intended things should go:
'Insurance necessary temporary expedient. At no distant date hope State will acknowledge full responsibility in the matter of making provision for sickness,

Above, the Labour Party on the terrace of the House of Commons in February, 1906, following its success at the polls when it became a political party of significance for the first time.

Right, sorting rubbish in London.

Far right, fishing for coal. The Lancashire poor devised this method of dredging the canal for lumps of coal dropped from passing lighters.

breakdown and unemployment. It really does so now, through Poor Law: but conditions under which this system had hitherto worked have been so harsh and humiliating that working-class pride revolts against accepting so degrading and doubtful a boon. Gradually the obligation of the State to find labour or sustenance will be realised and honourably interpreted.'

In spite of his confident assertion that his National Insurance Bill was non-controversial, it in fact aroused a good deal of opposition from disparate sections of the community. Socialists objected to it

because of the contributory element. Some doctors opposed it because they did not want to be dependent on the approved societies who were going to administer the insurance benefits (a point which was conceded in their favour). Other doctors opposed it because they felt the rates of remuneration were not good enough. Most remarkable of all among the objectors was what the popular press called the 'revolt of the duchesses', supported by their domestic servants and by the newspapers, including *The Times*. The 'duchesses' organised meetings in the Albert Hall to try to persuade the public not to stick stamps on the new 'bureaucratic and German' insurance cards (the British Government had studied the German insurance scheme before introducing its Bill). In spite of the opposition the Bill became law and the scheme came into operation in January, 1913. This social

**Above, morning on the fish-wharves at Yarmouth.
Right, a steam-hammer shaping a steel bar in a Sheffield steel-works.**

legislation, piecemeal and unco-ordinated as it was, set a pattern that has been followed in Britain ever since. But it was not enough to prevent the spread of unrest. At the time of his death in 1910 the King was as much concerned about the threat of domestic crisis as he was by the ominous trend of events abroad. Strikes were increasing in number and violence, and more people were resorting to direct action — both on behalf of discontented labour and for other causes. What had been ripples on the surface of Edwardian stability were to grow into deep and menacing waves in the years that bridged the gap between the King's death and the outbreak of the First World War.

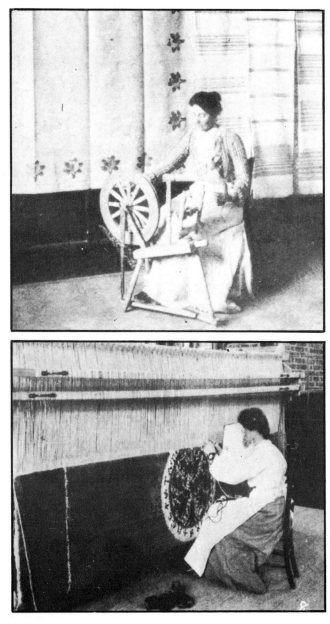

Top, the industrial garden city of Port Sunlight, built by Lever Brothers in the Wirral, was visited by the King and Queen in 1914, when the Queen watched packers at work in the scented-soap factory, above centre. Arts and crafts in traditional style were fostered in certain areas during Edwardian times, as demonstrated at the exhibition at Haslemere in 1905, left centre and bottom.

Right, the old-age Pensions Act came into operation in January, 1909, when pensioners went to the Post Office to receive their first instalments, which averaged 4s a week.

5 LEISURE

In pursuit of pleasure the Edwardian was a formidable figure. The whole-hearted attention he devoted to the appetites aroused by the table and the bed has already been noted, but his leisure interests were by no means confined to eating, drinking and making love. Sport and the arts flourished, and in many ways the Edwardian period was one of the most richly creative of the twentieth century so far. It was also far more widely informed, thanks to the rise of the popular press. In the nineteenth century daily newspapers such as *The Times* and serious weekly illustrated papers like *The Illustrated London News* were aimed mainly at the well-educated man with a reasonable amount of leisure time (perhaps at his club) in which to read them. It was Alfred Harmsworth who saw that the introduction of primary education for all in the nineteenth century had produced a demand for a different kind of newspaper, a 'busy man's paper', which gave succinct rather than lengthy reports of home and foreign news, broke up the columns of print with headings and sub-headings of varying sizes, with photographs rather than line drawings, and further stimulated readers' interest with items of gossip and controversy on minor matters of social behaviour and attitudes.

The first of the popular or 'family' papers was the *Daily Mail*, which Harmsworth launched in 1896 to sell at one halfpenny, and which was selling a million copies a day by the start of the new century. Arthur Pearson's *Daily Express* followed in 1900. Three years later followed the first tabloid, with even shorter stories, and the popular Sunday newspapers. Though he was a successful proprietor who knew how to sell newspapers Harmsworth, who became Lord Northcliffe in 1905, wanted more than commercial and journalistic success; he wanted power. Popular papers, in spite of their massive sales, could not give him this, so he

When Parliament reviewed the question of censorship of plays in 1909 they received deputations from authors and playwrights who included, top, J.M. Barrie (in bowler hat, carrying pipe) and Henry James, and, bottom, Harley Granville Barker (carrying umbrella).

Opposite page, top, G.K. Chesterton dressed as Dr Johnson for a church pageant. Chesterton wrote a weekly column for *The Illustrated London News*. Centre, Rudyard Kipling. Bottom, W. S. Gilbert.

Far right, Beerbohm Tree as Caliban in *The Tempest* at His Majesty's Theatre in 1904.

THE ILLUSTRATED
LONDON NEWS

REGISTERED AT THE GENERAL POST OFFICE AS A NEWSPAPER.

No. 3414.—VOL. CXXV. SATURDAY, SEPTEMBER 24, 1904. SIXPENCE.

The Copyright of all the Literary Matter, with Engravings and Letterpress, is Strictly Reserved in Great Britain, the Colonies, Europe, and the United States of America.

AWSON
WOOD /04

bought the *Observer* and installed J. L. Garvin as editor, and soon afterwards also bought *The Times*, whose circulation had fallen to around 38,000, but whose reputation and influence, as the newspaper best informed about the inner workings of British and foreign Governments, had survived. Northcliffe's purchase saved *The Times*, which was bankrupt, and his flair as a newspaperman brought many improvements to the paper. But his attempts to enforce his own political views on its editorial policies created havoc inside the office, and ensured, after his death in 1920, that future editors would be better protected from proprietorial interference.

One of Northcliffe's first acts when he took over control of *The Times* was to improve its coverage of the theatre, and here he showed great perception of what his readers wanted, for Edwardians loved the theatre. Both London and the provinces were well endowed with theatres, and with talented actors and actresses to perform in them. But going to a play was regarded as part of an evening's entertainment, and apart from Shakespeare serious drama was not what was generally wanted. As J. B. Priestley has noted, Edwardian theatre 'was almost as far removed from the mainstream of European drama as it would have been if it had been taken to Afghanistan.' Playwrights such as Ibsen, Strindberg and Chekhov did not easily fit in with the 'night out with the family' that tended to be the Edwardian approach to the theatre. So it would be, Priestley recalled, 'one of George Edwardes's Gaiety shows or one of those Viennese things, with all the waltzes, at Daly's; or a farce "adapted from the French" and just missing being "a bit too near the knuckle"; or one of the adorable laughter-and-tears pieces by Barrie; or another light comedy, very funny but just a wee bit sharp at times, by that very successful chap, Somerset Maugham.' (So successful was 'that chap' that at one time during the Edwardian period he had four plays running at the same time in the West End.)

The serious drama that Priestley pined for was represented by occasional performances by the Stage Society, and from 1904 by Harley Granville-Barker's productions at the Court Theatre, which he directed in close co-operation with George Bernard Shaw. Of

Above right, Dan Leno in *Mother Goose*, one of the pantomime hits at Drury Lane.

Right, Aino Ackte as Salome, at Covent Garden.

Far right, Adelina Patti, the soprano, singing to a crowded Albert Hall on her only London appearance in the 1901 season.

thirty-two plays put on at the Court between 1904 and 1907 there were eleven written by Shaw, including *Man and Superman* and *You Never Can Tell*. Granville-Barker was later to put on some memorable productions of Shakespeare, but the conventional productions (and there were plenty of them) tended to be treated as vehicles for the stars like Henry Irving, Beerbohm Tree, George Alexander and Johnston Forbes-Robertson, and were lavishly staged to the extent even of having live rabbits running about the forest of *A Midsummer Night's Dream*. The protagonists of the play with a purpose, or the Theatre of Ideas (as opposed to the Theatre Theatrical), which Shaw would say should be educational, deplored such spectacles, even when Shakespearian, and deplored also the drawing-room plays notable for their absence of thought. The ideas of men like Ibsen, wrote J. C. Trewin in his admirable account of the theatre of this period *The Edwardian Theatre* (1976), 'were taken more conveniently if they were warmed and filtered through the mind of Arthur Wing Pinero.'

Plays with purpose ran into difficulties with the censor, which was one of the reasons why commercial managements were wary of them. Richard Findlater has noted that of eight thousand plays submitted to the Lord Chamberlain's office between 1895 and 1909 only thirty were banned, but among those banned

Above left, Dame Nellie Melba in 1906.

Above, Nijinsky with Karsavina (left) and Schollar in *Jeux* at Drury Lane in 1913.

Right, Sir Henry Irving as Coriolanus, with Ellen Terry as Volumnia, at the Lyceum in 1901.

were plays by Shaw, Oscar Wilde, Granville-Barker, Ibsen, Tolstoy, Maeterlinck and Gerhardt Hauptmann. In spite of the campaign against censorship the Lord Chamberlain received plenty of support. One of the plays banned at this time was Granville-Barker's *Waste*, a play about a politician of promise whose career was wrecked by a brief affair with a woman. *The Times* commented on it in 1907; 'The subject matter of *Waste,* together with the sincere realism with which it is treated, makes it in our judgment wholly unfit for performance, under ordinary conditions, before a miscellaneous public of various ages, moods and standards of intelligence ' When, in 1909, a Joint Select Committee of the Houses of Lords and Commons met to review the question of censorship they drew on a strong cast of witnesses. Among the playwrights who gave evidence were Shaw, Granville-Barker, John Galsworthy, Pinero, and W. S. Gilbert; among the actor-managers were Tree, Alexander, and

Forbes-Robertson; among the critics were William Archer and A. B. Walkley. The managers and some actors gave evidence in support of the Examiner of Plays, the writers were vehement in his denunciation. A good many of those who gave evidence on both sides took the opportunity to put on a histrionic performance that was not always relevant to the subject under review. In the end the Lord Chamberlain was charged with maintaining his role of protecting the public from any play which in his opinion was not conducive to the presentation of good manners, decorum or the public peace, though he was pronounced free to reconsider his ban on any play at any time should he feel so disposed.

More popular than the drama, and not too concerned about good manners or decorum, were the music halls and variety shows inherited from the Victorian era. In Edwardian times the variety houses were scattered all over London, the suburbs and the provinces. The shows were twice nightly, and they usually included acrobats and jugglers, conjurors and illusionists, male impersonators like Vesta Tilley, drolls like Little Tich and Dan Leno, comedians like George Robey and Harry Tate, and entertainers like the inimitable Marie Lloyd. With performers of this quality the Edwardian music hall flourished, and few who patronised it with such evident enthusiasm can have appreciated that this form of entertainment was already approaching its end. Yet the principal cause of its destruction was already being incorporated in variety's own programmes, for many of them were closing their bills with a few minutes of jerky and silent film, then called the Bioscope. J. B. Priestley has recalled that in his youth he and his friends seldom bothered to stay on to see the film, but in this he was unusual. By 1914 more and more music halls were being converted into picture palaces, more than 200 companies had registered with the Board of Trade as film exhibitors, and more than 3,500 cinemas were already in existence.

Writers, musicians and painters all contributed to the reputation for creativity that the Edwardian age enjoyed. The educated middle classes were stimulated in these interests not only by the spread of newspapers and magazines but also by the introduction of cheap reprints of classics in series such as Dent's Everyman's Library and the Oxford University Press's World's Classics, and by the growth of the circulating libraries. Bernard Shaw, though he had celebrated his fiftieth birthday in 1906, was one of the leaders of the 'younger' writers who were regarded with unease by many Edwardians because they challenged established Victorian values, and because they lived and worked, even when they were not deliberately challenging such

An advertisement for the Great Northern Railway that appeared in *The Illustrated London News* in July 1907.

Above right, mixed bathing in August, 1910.

Right, roller-skaters on the pier-rink at Bournemouth.

Far right, a beauty contest at Folkestone in 1910. The winner and five runners-up went forward to compete against foreign beauty queens in an international contest, though she was not at that time given the title of "Miss World".

values, in an atmosphere of what Priestley has described as 'hopeful debate' — ready to argue, in public and in private, convinced that they had only to win the intellectual argument to ensure that society would be rationally transformed. Many writers both stimulated and were themselves stimulated by the atmosphere of inquiry that pervaded the times, including G. K. Chesterton (who, in 1905, took over the writing of the weekly 'Our Notebook' feature in *The Illustrated London News,* which he continued to write until his death in 1936), H. G. Wells, Thomas Hardy, Joseph Conrad, D. H. Lawrence, Arnold Bennett, John Galsworthy, Max Beerbohm, Hilaire Belloc, W. H. Hudson and Kenneth Grahame. Many of them reflected their comments on their lives and times most potently in the form of novels, particularly Lawrence and Wells. Lawrence was charged with obscenity, and *Ann Veronica,* Wells's novel about a courageous but 'forward' Edwardian woman, was banned from the libraries and condemned by many contemporary critics for the particular offence, as Wells himself put it, that Ann Veronica 'was a virgin who fell in love and showed it, instead of waiting, as all popular heroines had hitherto done, for someone to make love to her. It was held to be an unspeakable offence that an adolescent female should be sex-conscious before the thing was forced on her attention.' Edwardians frequently found new things unspeakable, which should not seem surprising when it is remembered that they were brought up to be conventional Victorians and were constantly being surprised, angered and probably more than a little frightened by books, paintings and music that seemed to undermine all that they had been taught to respect.

In art the moment of confrontation for Edwardians is generally taken to have been the Grafton Galleries exhibition of post-Impressionists, organised by Roger Fry in 1910, though in fact the Cezannes, Van Goghs, and Gaugins that caused such uncomprehending ribaldry and apoplexy among visitors to the gallery had mostly been painted in the previous decade. The new painters who were to become so influential in the Edwardian and post-Edwardian times were Picasso, Braque and Matisse, the first two joining forces in 1909 to develop Cubism. The English artists of the period were less revolutionary, the most influential being Walter Sickert, who founded the Camden Town Group (later called the London Group) in 1910, and the more fashionable John Singer Sargent.

In music the Edwardians could boast of ten years of intense creativity, having the giant Elgar at the height of his powers as well as Delius, Vaughan Williams and Gustav Holst. They also enjoyed the conducting of Sir Henry Wood, whose promenade

Above, the London Season: the King and Queen at the Duchess of Wellington's ball at Apsley House in July, 1908. *The Illustrated London News* **announced that this was the first time the King had been portrayed as a dancer.**

Right, the popular dance: the summer theatre at Earls Court was turned into a ballroom in 1908, and quickly became a popular centre for dancing.

concerts had started in 1895, and Sir Thomas Beecham, who began his career as conductor of the New Symphony Orchestra in 1906, and the playing of such orchestras as the London Symphony Orchestra, which gave its first concert at the Queen's Hall in 1904. Another distinguished musical achievement was the collection of English folk songs by Cecil Sharp, traditional music that was then on the verge of extinction. For the musically inclined the revolutionary elements that summoned up the blood pressure of the conventional were provided in the main by Igor Stravinsky, whose first symphony was performed in 1907 and whose international reputation quickly spread following performances of *The Firebird* and *Petrushka* by the Diaghilev ballet company in 1910

and 1911, and the publication of *The Rite of Spring* in 1913. The Diaghilev company visited Britain for the first time in 1911, when it gave several performances at Covent Garden, with Beecham conducting.

For most Edwardians, however, the popular music was that which they heard in the music halls and on the musical comedy stage; and it was these numbers which they sang with such exuberance when they went on 'outings', which for many were the only holidays that could be afforded, or the only opportunity to get away from the town or village where they lived and worked. The outing was organised by the office or factory, or by a local women's organisation or school, or by a club or other social group. Flora Thompson described those organised in Candleford Green:

'In summer there were the "outings". That of the Mothers' Meeting, after weeks of discussion of more or less desirable seaside resorts, always decided for London and the Zoo. The Choir Outing left in the small hours of the morning for Bournemouth or Weston-super-Mare; and the Children's School Treat Outing went, waving flags and singing, in a horse wagonette to the village paddock in a neighbouring village, where tea and buns were partaken of at a long trestle table under some trees. After tea they ran races and played games, and returned home, tired and grubby, but still noisy, to find even a larger crowd than had seen them off waiting on the green to welcome them and join in their "Hip-hip-hooray!"'

Here is a description from Alan Delgado's *The Annual Outing and Other Excursions* (1977), of an outing of W. H. Smith's Warehouse (Printing Department) in Fetter Lane, London, which took place on June 26, 1909:

'The destination was the Ship Inn at Eastcote near Pinner. Catching the 1 pm train from Marylebone they arrived at Pinner and strolled through some of the finest country in Middlesex to the Ship Inn at Eastcote where they were welcomed by their host, Mr Silvester. The extensive grounds of the Ship Inn were explored and after a splendid dinner the party adjourned to a cricket field and watched an exciting match, Married Men v Single Men. The Single Men won by three runs. Having survived the suspense of the match the party sat down to a tea which was all that could be desired. Then came the last event, a concert to which several members contributed, the star turn being a Mr Matts's rendering of "She's My Daisy". The health of the chairman having been drunk with musical honours, he proceeded to wind up the evening with a neat little

Polo at Hurlingham: the French artist J. Simont painted this impression of a contest in the Inter-Regimental Tournament in 1910.

speech entitled "Our Department". Having said "au revoir" to the host, the party caught the 10.47 pm train back to London.'

Many outings had the seaside as their destination, for the Edwardians carried on the Victorian enthusiasm for excursions and longer holidays beside the sea. Southend was rapidly developing as a resort for the day tripper and holidaymaker from London's east end (its population increased from 29,000 in 1901 to 63,000 in 1911), as was Blackpool for those who lived in the industrial north-west. The railways and charabancs and motor cars brought the sea within easy reach, but already to some the disadvantages were becoming apparent. A doctor wrote in *The Illustrated London News* of his unhappy holiday experience in 1903:

'The other day I tried to enjoy a holiday in a seaside resort. Time was when you could escape from the pressure of work, and pass some quiet, delightful hours by the waves. Now all is altered wherever one goes. The motor cars fizz and roar by the dozen. They monopolise every road and street, and are propelled in towns at a pace which if represented in the case of a horse-carriage would certainly entail a prosecution for furious driving. The motor car is no doubt a useful machine, and may come to replace our horse vehicles, but it will have to be controlled as to speed and noise if we are to enjoy life. A motor "neurosis" is being developed in our midst, both on the part of people who motor and of those who have to scramble out of the motorist's way. All this develops the spirit of unrest and hurry. The man who motors knows he can spurt at thirty or forty miles an hour, and this develops in him the hustling neurosis. Similarly, if to cross a thoroughfare I have to bethink myself of a chance of sudden death through a motorist who regards the road as peculiarly his own, I am in similar danger of becoming a nervous person in spite of myself.'

For those who could afford it the cross-Channel steamers brought the continent of Europe also within the bounds of holiday-making. A woman's magazine gave some practical advice to its readers about the problem of winter sporting:

'There has been a great deal written lately about winter sport and Swiss holidays generally, but there is always so much taken for granted, and Mrs Tenderfoot, who has never been before, and does not know anyone very intimately who has, wants to be told all about it from the very beginning, for, as she remarks naively ,"I don't even know where to go to get snow, and I don't want to just exchange English mud for Swiss."

'Having decided the prospect is attractive, she feels

On the river. Top, a tow from a passing barge saves effort. Bottom, the 1906 university boat race seen from Barnes Bridge, with Cambridge, who eventually won, in the lead.

Left, golf was among the sports in which the King took a practical interest.
Centre, Miss Thompson, ladies' golf champion, driving in the 1906 tournament.

The former Prime Minister, Arthur Balfour, in play against the former champion, Harry Vardon (in peaked cap, holding club), at Knebworth in 1908.

Taking service in "Il Diabolo". The game, a great craze in the nineteenth century, had a revival of popularity in mid-Edwardian times.

Queen Alexandra playing billiards with her sister, the Dowager-Empress of Russia, at the Villa Hvidore, the Queen's Danish home near Copenhagen.

she could "quite well organise such a trip", but what is it likely to cost? It depends of course on how much this particular Mrs Tenderfoot has to spend. But there are second-class return tickets available for 60 days for about £6. She could reckon on being taken at a hotel for 10 shillings a day, with a considerable reduction for children; she could go to a pension for 2 guineas a week, or even take rooms at a chalet for less than that.

'The sound thing for Mrs Tenderfoot to do is to tackle the budget and see what she has to spend, then choose her place and decide how long she will stay; and let her remember at the same time that the Christmas holidays are expensive at home, and there will be a lot of pleasure, and health thrown in, if she decides to spend them abroad.'

Such holidays were for the few. Sport, either playing or watching or, with the advent of the popular press, for simply reading about, was for all. It was becoming the most popular relaxation, and sporting metaphors abounded in all walks of life. 'He'll make a capital king', said a huntsman of Edward when he was Prince of Wales, 'He sits a horse so well.' Edward when he became king was a keen sportsman, mostly as a spectator, and his enthusiasm for horse racing in particular was shared by a good many of his subjects, as they demonstrated at Epsom in 1909 when his colt

Above, athletic English women playing ice hockey during a brief icy spell in 1907. Below, moonlight tobogganing on Parliament Hill, Hampstead.

110

Top, the Edwardian craze for roller-skating led women to play football on them.

Bottom, an exhibition of women's fencing skills in 1902.

Minoru won the Derby by a short head, the first horse to win this classic race for a reigning monarch. The King's other principal sporting enthusiasm, yachting, was not so widely shared, though *The Illustrated London News* and other news magazines regularly recorded the racing at Cowes and the battles for the America's Cup. The King lent his support to many other sports in which he was less personally involved. He opened the Olympic Games of 1908, which were held at the White City in London, and Queen Alexandra presented the medals, including a special gold cup to the Italian marathon runner Durando Pietri, who was disqualified after he had collapsed when in the lead and been helped across the finish. The public attended the Games in vast numbers, and lined the course of the marathon from Windsor to the stadium, and their confidence in Britain's superiority was confirmed by the results, which have never since been equalled. Britain won a total of fifty-six gold medals, America came second with twenty-two and Sweden third with eight. In the rowing section of the Games, held at Henley, Britain won all five events, including one in which the British four had sportingly waited for their Dutch opponents to resume rowing after their boat had run into the booms lining the course. For the general public rowing was normally of interest only at the time of the university boat race, at which time virtually the whole nation seemed to divide evenly, and with surprising fervour, between the light and dark blues, and many thousands of spectators crowded the banks of the Thames to catch

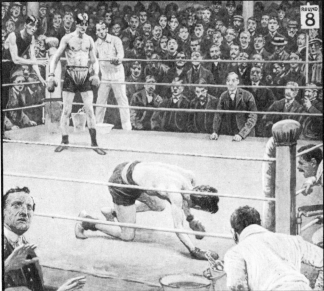

Top, wrestling became a popular spectator sport in Edwardian times. Here Ahmed Madrali, the "Terrible Turk", is thrown by Georges Hackenschmidt, the "Russian Lion", in the first seconds of a bout watched by 10,000 spectators at Olympia.

Bottom, boxing was generally regarded as a disreputable sport in Edwardian times, but there was no shortage of boxers nor of opportunities to watch them fight. One of the outstanding boxers of the period was Bombardier Billy Wells, who retained the national heavyweight title for nine years.

Top, the Cup Final of 1901, played between Tottenham Hotspur and Sheffield United at the Crystal Palace, resulted in a draw, 2–2. The game was watched by more than 100,000 people.

Bottom, the New Zealand All-Blacks rugby football team beat England in the third test at the Crystal Palace in 1905 by 15 points to nil. Only one team, Wales, managed to beat the All-Blacks during their successful tour, in the course of which they amassed 830 points against 39.

a glimpse of the boats as they went by. Honours during this period were almost even — of the fifteen races between 1900 and 1914 Cambridge won eight and Oxford seven.

Other games developed both as social pastimes and as competitive international events during Edwardian times, including lawn tennis, golf, hockey and rugby football, but none built up the support and popular interest so much as association football in the winter months and cricket in the summer. Association football dominated the industrial north and the midlands, and the number of spectators seemed to increase every Saturday. The first cup final, played at the Oval in 1872, had been watched by some 2,000 people. The cup final of 1901, which was played at the Crystal Palace, was seen by more than 100,000. At the start of the century eight thousand clubs were registered with the Football Association, and of these three hundred were professional. The game had become commercial enough by 1905 for a Middlesborough player to be transferred to Sunderland for £1,000. But soccer was not by any means dominated by the professional game at this time: in many respects the leading club was not one of the great professionals, like Aston Villa or Sunderland, but the Corinthians, an amateur team whose players were drawn mainly from Oxford and Cambridge. In the annual match between the leading amateur and the leading professional clubs the Corinthians frequently won. In 1904 they beat Bury (who had won the cup without conceding a goal and the cup final by the record score of 6-0 against Derby County) by the remarkable score of 10-3.

On the first Saturday in May each year Association Football gave way uncomplainingly to cricket as the prime sporting preoccupation. Though the great Dr W. G. Grace had retired from the first class game in 1900, the Edwardian summers nonetheless provided a feast of cricket. There were now sixteen first class counties, and there were many great cricketers who met the demand of large crowds with such prodigality, as John Arlott has suggested in his essay on Edwardian sport in *Edwardian England*, as can surely never be repeated:
'The entertainment they offered was the unfailing delight of the cricket watcher — a profusion of runs, handsomely scored . . . The circumstances were ideal. The rough grounds of fifty years earlier had given way to strips marled to perfection, defying the skills of all but a few bowlers to wrest pace or turn from them. In such a setting stroke-players flourished through what appears, in the recollection of those who played in it and from the records of the time, to have been an age of sunshine and true, fast pitches. Of course there were

The Thermos flask, an Edwardian invention, was widely advertised in the early 1900s as an essential accompaniment for all outdoor occasions.

Right, cricket was the Edwardian sportsman's prime summer preoccupation. Those who went to Lord's on July 1, 1907, were lucky enough to see one of Gilbert Jessop's great innings. Going in when England had scored only 158 runs for five in the first Test Match against South Africa, he scored 93 in little over an hour.

sticky wickets, and of course bowlers had their days, but the main picture is of batsmen lording it in a summertime of runs.'

With players to watch like Hobbs, Ranjitsinhji, C. B. Fry, MacLaren, Tyldesley and Spooner, Jessop and Jackson Hirst and Rhodes, Woolley and S. F. Barnes, it was perhaps during the cricket season that the Edwardian period came nearest to deserving its nostalgic label of the 'golden age'.

JESSOP'S IMPARTIAL 93.

AUTOGRAPH HUNTERS.

THE INEVITABLE TELEGRAPH BOY.

DR GRACE INSPECTING THE WICKET.

THE IDOL OF THE CROWD, JESSOP.

THE TWO CAPTAINS P.W. SHERWELL, S.A. (LEFT) R.E. FOSTER, ENG. (RIGHT).

HAYWARD & FRY BATTING.

The first Olympic Games ever to be held in Britain were opened at Shepherd's Bush Stadium in July 1908. The sensation of the games was the finish of the marathon in which Dorando Pietri, the Italian athlete, right, entered the stadium first. He was utterly exhausted, and collapsed before completing the final lap. He was helped towards the tape and crossed first, but was disqualified and Queen Alexandra, who was watching, later presented him with a gold cup as consolation. Among other events at the games, far right, from top, were bicycle polo, a three-mile team race, the high jump and the 100 metres (won by the Englishman, M. Chapman, in 11.2 seconds).

6 YOUNG EDWARDIANS

When the first nursery school was opened in January, 1900, in Deptford, the event was described as heralding the dawn of the 'children's century'. Cynics have not failed to point out that those children who were of an age to go to nursery school at the start of the century were old enough to fight in the First World War, and if they were lucky enough to survive and return to have a family of their own then the probability was that their children would have had to fight in the second. It has not been quite the century that the confident Edwardians had hoped for, but they nonetheless made great advances in providing for the care and education of children. The passing of the Education Act of 1902, devised by Sir Robert Morant, an official of the Board of Education, and sponsored in Parliament by Mr Arthur Balfour, reorganised elementary and secondary education and laid the foundations of the modern State educational system in Britain. That there was need for change had been made clear by the Bryce Report on Secondary Education in 1895, which concluded that the old system of trying to do as much as possible by voluntary effort was no longer adequate for an advanced industrial nation. 'We cannot refuse to strengthen the hold of the State upon our education,' said a member of the Bryce Commission. 'Irresistible forces drive us on. We are in the suck of a strong current. Act we must, because other nations with whom we have to compete, not only in the sphere of industry and commerce, but in the momentous struggle between national ideals, have thrown themselves with all their energy into the work of educational reconstruction.'

In 1900 the Board of Education was set up, and in 1902 the Education Act gave to county and county boroughs the responsibility of all secondary and technical education, including voluntary schools (though these retained control over the appointment of teachers in exchange for providing the buildings), so that public money was thus provided to ensure a basic level of education for all children. The same benefits were also to be applied to elementary schools. The Act was passed after fifty-nine days of debate, and in the teeth of fierce opposition from Nonconformists, who demanded a system of undenominational schools in place of the mainly Church of England schools which, in rural areas, were often the only ones available, and who objected strongly to the idea of subsidising sectarian schools on the rates. They

A breath of fresh air for a party of children brought down from London in 1903 for their first sight of the sea.

campaigned, using the slogan 'The Church on the Rates', for years after the Act was passed, and formed a National Passive Resistance Committee, under the leadership of the Baptist minister Dr John Clifford. In spite of their attempts to organise a mass refusal to pay education rates which led to many legal actions, the protests were never strong enough to affect the working of the new education system, which in essence provided a State ladder by which able children could rise from primary to secondary education. That the Act of 1902 (and a similar one for London passed in the following year) took an important step towards providing the country with the better-educated people it badly needed is made clear from the figures for the number of pupils in grant-aided secondary schools, which increased from 94,000 in 1905 to 156,000 in 1910 and to 200,000 in 1914.

In 1907 the Liberal Government introduced the 'free place' system, under which secondary schools which did not reserve one quarter of their places, free of fees, for children educated in public elementary schools were to receive a lower State grant. This broadened the ladder of advancement from primary to secondary education, but though equality of opportunity in education was a common theme of Edwardian social reformers, it was not in this period common practice, and less than one fifth of Edwardian boys reached a secondary school of any kind. Of these most would be middle class, though less than half of middle class Edwardian boys attended a secondary school; for working class boys the proportion was less than 10 per cent. The compulsory school age remained at 12, and was not raised to 14 until 1918. Nonetheless education was given much higher priority than it had been; between 1902 and 1913 educational spending by local authorities increased from £9 million to £30 million, and that of the central government from £12 million to £19 million.

The public schools did not accept financial aid from public authorities, but the new competition from State secondary education was far from injurious; indeed, the public schools entered a new era of prosperity in Edwardian times. They were, however, not very adventurous in responding to the mood of the times. Robert Cecil has suggested that they were, by and large, 'strongholds of educational complacency and conservatism' because Oxford and Cambridge universities were the same, though there were some enlightened dons and schoolmasters who recognised the need to rethink the nineteenth-century concept of the aim of education. He pointed out, in *Life in Edwardian England* (1969), that 'Then, as now, the root question was whether education should seek to produce a man who could use in his career the know-

PROBLEM OF THE DAY—THE EDUCATION BIL

Children in a London Board School.

Above, children in a London Board School in 1908. Above right, a demonstration in the Albert Hall against the Education Bill—one of a number introduced during the Edwardian era that laid the foundation of the modern State educational system in Britain. Right, children in an LCC school in the East End in 1911 being taught how to fill in census forms so that they could help their parents, many of whom were illiterate.

ledge he had acquired, or whether the object was to train a mind and character which would respond afterwards to the stresses of life. If we criticise the Edwardians for allowing this important debate to degenerate, as it tended to do, into a stereotyped argument about the benefits of a classical, as against a scientific and more modern education, we must remember how difficult it was for them to envisage the environment for which young people were being prepared. Their world was changing with bewildering rapidity, and the wisest could not foresee what the future might hold.'

For the most part Edwardian public schools inherited, and accepted without too much question, the educational ideas of Dr Arnold, the headmaster of Rugby, summed up as the three c's of classics, cricket and Christianity. However, although there

were those who questioned the wisdom of devoting such obsessive attention to *Amo, Mensa* and *Hic haec hoc* and to 'playing the game', there was no widespread move to follow the lead in progressive education set by Abbotsholme, which had been founded at the end of the nineteenth century. The headmaster of Abbotsholme, Dr Cecil Reddie, aimed to provide a wider, more balanced and more inter-denominational curriculum than was the custom in public schools. 'The school does not undertake to prepare boys for competitive exams,' he wrote in 1913, 'owing to the fact that these exams require specialisation too much at the expense of a more broadly educative curriculum . . . There is no modern side, and no classical side, and, therefore, no one-sidedness. A liberal education is regarded as not having sides.' Dr Reddie's ideas marked the beginning of the end of the strict adherence to Arnoldian tradition. Other schools, notably Bedales, Oundle, Loretto, The Perse, and Gresham's, were working their own ways towards more progressive styles of education during the years before the First World War, but these were exceptional and most public schools remained fairly traditional in outlook — with emphasis on classics and games and such character-building activities as cold baths, fagging and corporal punishment.

Higher education in Edwardian times was an even more exclusive preoccupation. At the start of the century there were no more than 20,000 students receiving full-time education in British universities, and there were far fewer universities in this country than there were overseas. In 1903 the President of the British Association, Norman Lockyer, complained that Germany had 22 universities, and gave more state aid to one of them than was received by all the 13 universities in Britain. The United States by this time had 134 universities, and Italy with 21 and France with 15 also had more than Britain. Conservative and complacent though they may have been, both Oxford and Cambridge universities made progressive changes during this period. Oxford benefited from the arrival, in 1907, of Lord Curzon as Chancellor, for under his leadership a considerable amount of academic reform was put into effect, and Cambridge was already the centre of some remarkable scientific work in spite of its lack of teaching facilities in some of the sciences. Nonetheless, it was evidently the case that many undergraduates at the two senior universities were not too concerned about

Top, Fulham Council, unable to take the children to the sea, did its best to bring the seaside to the children in 1903 by collecting sand from Ramsgate and flooding an extension of Fulham Park. Bottom, at the entrance to Blackwall Tunnel the London County Council set up a sandpit for East End children.

Under the provisions of the Children Act of 1909 no child was allowed into a bar where alcoholic drink was being consumed. Some landlords set aside a room where children could wait, others would not allow them in at all. At the Black Horse, Catford, nurses were stationed outside to look after the children while their parents were inside.

the need to acquire good degrees. Sport was practised with even greater intensity than at the public schools. The Master of Magdalen, Oxford, revealed that of those who went up in 1909 a quarter did not take a degree, and deduced from their attitude that most of them had come up to have a good time rather than to read or work hard, while Sir Reader Bullard has recalled that he was surprised to find that, in the same period, undergraduates at Queen's, Cambridge, 'were drifting through their Pass Degree, which made no great demands on their time and energy'.

More striking, perhaps, than developments at the two older universities during Edward's reign was the growth of new universities. In 1900 Mason College, Birmingham, had obtained a charter as Birmingham University — the first example of a large industrial city having a university of its own. In the same year London University was issued with statutes giving it for the first time the framework of a modern academic organisation which comprised not just University, King's and Bedford Colleges but in addition ten medical schools, six theological colleges, the London School of Economics, the South-Eastern Agricultural College, and the Central Technical College of the City and Guilds Institution. In 1903 the three constituent colleges of Victoria University — Manchester, Liverpool and Leeds — were each formed into separate universities. Manchester and Liverpool received their charters in 1903, and Leeds in the following year. In 1905 Sheffield University came into being, to be followed in 1909 by Bristol. By 1914 there were in addition six institutions ranking as university colleges outside London — Exeter, Newcastle, Nottingham, Reading, Southampton and the Manchester School of Technology.

The Early Edwardian confidence that this was to be the children's century was supported to some extent by the legislation they introduced outside the realm of formal education, and which collectively came to be known as the 'children's charter'. The introduction of nursery schools has already been noted. Two years later, as a first step towards reducing the high rate of infant mortality, a measure to compel the registration of midwives was introduced. Provision for school meals was made in 1906, and in 1907 the Board of Education established its own medical department. Special schools were set up to provide for incapacitated children, and Juvenile Courts, Probation Officers and Borstals were established as an alternative to the former system of treating young offenders as criminals. But measures to reduce infant mortality, to improve the health of children of school age, and to treat delinquents in rather more humane a fashion, only tackled one part of the problem; they did not of themselves

The Boy Scout movement was founded by Sir Robert (later Lord) Baden-Powell in 1907. By 1911 it had grown to such a size that 40,000 scouts joined a rally in Windsor Great Park for inspection by the King.

A union jack formed by six thousand boys at Sheffield on Empire Day, 1906.

In August, 1908, the King's grandsons, Prince Edward and Prince Albert, visited the Franco-British Exhibition at the White City, in London, and made four trips on the scenic railway.

The two Princes were keen cyclists, as were so many Edwardians. In 1902 they took their bicycles, received as birthday presents from the King, to the Windsor and Eton regatta.

 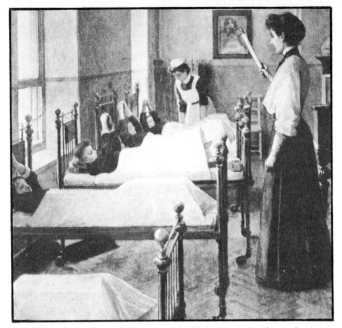

change the fundamental parental attitudes towards the upbringing and treatment of children. These attitudes were inherited from the Victorian era, and tended to vacillate, in Robert Cecil's words, 'between an undiscerning faith in childish innocence and an equally misguided determination to treat disobedient children as sons of Belial'. Rigorous discipline at home, where the rule of law was exercised without right of appeal by the usually rather remote head of the household, was backed up by the readily exercised discipline of the cane at school. The rules of conduct were well-defined and clearly understood, which had the not inconsiderable advantage for a child of providing a sense of stability and security in the home. But the Edwardian age was not just an extension of the Victorian, and the restlessness of the age, the improvements in education, the recognition of the need for change, even the welcome improvements brought about by the 'children's charter', all began to exert a change in attitudes towards youth — a process which was to be radically speeded up by the experience of war.

Meanwhile a movement grew up which was not designed to bring about a dramatic change, but which in a very short time succeeded in doing so by capturing the interest and enthusiasm of young people all over the world in a way that had never before been achieved or thought possible. This was the Boy Scout movement, which was launched by Sir Robert, later Lord, Baden-Powell in 1907. Baden-Powell had for some years been interested in the Boys' Brigade, a movement started in 1880 which gave boys the opportunity to drill and parade like miniature soldiers. Drawing on his experience at the seige of Mafeking, when he had organised boys to carry out useful jobs, Baden-Powell concluded that the scout was a better model than the soldier. In 1906 he published his book *Scouting for Boys* in which he declared that the country was suffering from the growth of 'shirkers' — men who shirked their duties and responsibilities to the State, and to others. He gave the scouts the motto 'Be Prepared', and set out to train them to use their powers of observation, to learn simple and useful skills, to be patriotic, to be helpful to others, and to get out into the open air. He described in his book how he had seen 'thousands of boys and young men, pale, narrow-chested, hunched-up, miserable specimens, smoking endless cigarettes', and he wanted to make them active and healthy, and 'to help existing organisations in making the rising generation, of whatever class or creed, into good citizens or useful colonists.' In 1907 the first Scout camp was set up, and in 1909 11,000 boy scouts paraded at the Crystal Palace. At this rally Baden-Powell saw a group of girls who had organised themselves, and he quickly enrolled them to become the first Girl Guides. By the following year well over 100,000 scouts had enrolled in troops all over Britain, and the movement spread rapidly throughout Europe and the Empire, and eventually throughout the civilised world.

In July, 1905, the King opened the new University of Sheffield, one of eleven new universities set up in the country during the Edwardian era, though Britain still lagged behind America, France and Germany in providing for higher education.

Making words.

Laying the tables.

Biscuits for lunch.

Ladies first.

Graded silks. For training colour sense.

Tidying up after lunch.

Bow tying.

A few minutes "go as you please."

The Montessori method of teaching aroused great interest in Edwardian England, and in 1914 *The Illustrated London News* **published this diagram to explain the system which promised, the magazine said, "to upset the old-**

Walking the chalk line

Silence, followed by silent moving of chairs.

Balance walking

Distinguishing different materials by touch.

The long stair.

Geometric insets

Wooden insets

S.BECK

fashioned and rather laborious method under which children are frequently taught to read and write".

Edwardians were keen photographers, and the Queen was among the most enthusiastic. She brought out her camera when the royal yacht sailed into Cartagena in 1907, top left. One of the imaginative photographic ideas of the times was to strap a camera to a pigeon to gain aerial photographs of enemy territory, top right. One of the most popular cameras of the day for ordinary use was the Kodak folding pocket camera, inset. Bottom, an early example of photography from the air—Buckingham Palace seen from a balloon.

An international balloon race was held in 1909. The photograph was taken as some of the balloons prepared for the start at Hurlingham.

The first motor-driven aircraft was flown by Wilbur and Orville Wright at Kitty Hawk, North Carolina, on December 17, 1903, when the machine flew for 59 seconds and reached a speed of 30 mph, In 1908, when this photograph was taken, Wilbur Wright flew a later version of his aeroplane for an hour and 31 minutes.

Top, a drawing of the Wright Brother's aeroplane published in *The Illustrated London News* in 1908 under the heading "Wright's secret of flying revealed at last". Bottom, in 1909 King Edward visited Pau, in France, to see the aircraft in flight and to have its details explained to him by Wilbur Wright.

In July, 1909, Louis Blériot dented Edwardian self-confidence by becoming the first man to fly the channel. The photograph shows Blériot beside his aircraft after landing on the cliffs of Dover.

The first fatal air crash in England occurred in July, 1910, when C. S. Rolls, seen at the controls of his aircraft, above, was killed when the machine suddenly went out of control and fell 50 feet to the ground, top.

As flying developed men began to concern themselves about safety, and in 1912 *The Illustrated London News* published a drawing of a parachute which, though described as "somewhat fantastic", was nonetheless regarded as a method "within the bounds of possibility".

Top, in 1905 the War Office ordered the construction of the biggest airship then known, the Barton-Rawson vessel, which was 150 feet long. It was launched from Alexandra Palace on July 22, but was virtually destroyed on landing near Romford.

Bottom, the saloon of the first passenger airship *Deutschland,* which made its maiden flight in 1910.

The sea-plane with folding wings, made by Short, was introduced in 1914. It was designed to save hangar-space and to be carried on battleships. Top, the plane with wings closed, bottom, with left wing half open and right wing in flying position. Top speed was 70 mph.

7 YEARS OF UNREST (1910-1914)

When the King's horse won the Derby in 1909 one of the enthusiastic crowd who threw their hats in the air with cries of 'Good old Teddy!' shouted out to him: 'Now King. You've won the Derby. Go back home and dissolve this bloody Parliament!' The King laughed heartily because, as Philip Magnus has suggested, he was 'disgusted with his Government and dismayed by a sudden and unprecedented rise in the nation's political temperature'. The Government referred to was a Liberal one led by Asquith, who had succeeded Campbell-Bannerman as Prime Minister on the latter's death in 1908. Asquith had brought in Lloyd George as Chancellor of the Exchequer and put Winston Churchill at the Board of Trade, and faced with the necessity of raising money to pay not only for their social reforms but also for naval rearmament the Government devised a 'People's Budget' that introduced supertax, a duty of 20 per cent on the 'unearned increment of land value' to be paid whenever land changed hands, and taxes on petrol and motor licences.

The 1909 Budget was, to say the least, controversial, and as Lloyd George had expected raised the greatest opposition among landowners, many of whom sat in the House of Lords. Meetings for and against the budget were held all over the country and the fact that many of the protest meetings were presided over by Dukes gave the Chancellor the opportunity to observe that a 'fully-equipped Duke costs as much to keep up as two dreadnoughts', and that a Duke was less easy to scrap. The House of Lords rejected the budget, after six days of debate, by 350 votes to 75, and this inevitably precipitated a general election. When this took place in January, 1910, the Liberals were returned with 275 seats, a loss of 104, but the Conservative Unionists won only 273, and the Liberals could count on the support of 40 Labour Party members and most of the 82 Irish Nationalists to secure their majority. Following the election result the Lords let the budget go through (though the land taxes were not implemented as originally planned), but the constitutional issue remained because the Government was now determined to secure the passage of its Parliament Bill, which it introduced in April, 1910, whether the Lords approved it or not. Under the Bill all control over Money Bills was removed from the second chamber, and it was left to the Speaker of the House of Commons to decide which Bills were Money Bills. The delaying power of

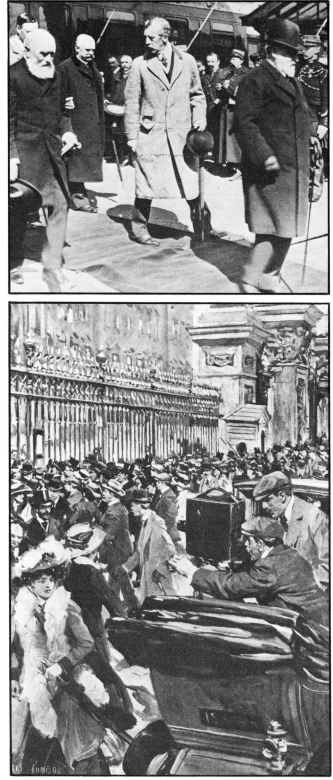

Top, on April 27, 1910, the King left Calais to return to London from Biarritz, where he had been staying for six weeks. He had not been well, and on May 6, as anxious crowds gathered outside the gates of Buckingham Palace, bottom, he collapsed and died.

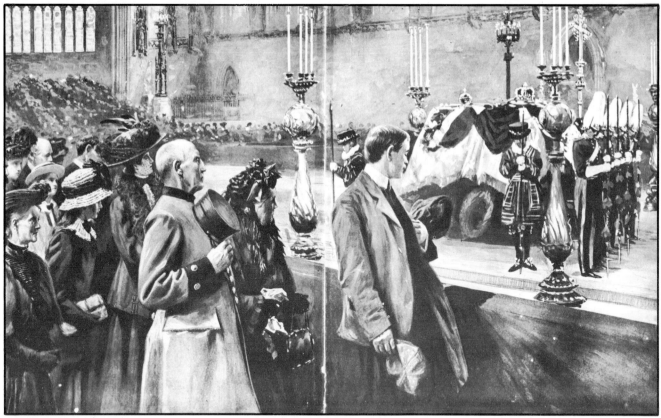

The popular grief that swept the nation at the news of King Edward's death was reflected in the number of his subjects who queued outside Westminster Hall to file past his coffin.

The Prince of Wales kneels in homage before King George V at the Coronation of the new King in 1911.

the Lords was reduced to two years, and the maximum life of Parliament was shortened from seven years to five.

The issue of Parliamentary reform brought the Crown into the centre of politics, for the question now was whether or not the King would be prepared to agree to the appointment of more than 400 peers to ensure the passage of the Bill if the House of Lords rejected it. King Edward was distressed both at the Crown's involvement and at the divisions that he saw opening up in society as a result of the vehemence of the debates first on the budget and now on the constitutional crisis. He regretted, on the one hand, attempts 'to inflame the passions of the working and lower orders against the people who happen to be the owners of property', of which he thought some of his Ministers had been guilty, and, on the other, the provocative statements made by opponents of the Government, who accused it of planning a social revolution. Among the latter must certainly be included Lord Willoughby de Broke, a Tory peer and master of foxhounds, who wrote in his memoirs that 'the order of battle was now fairly set for a campaign of class warfare'. He offered himself as a recruit, and toured the country making speeches defending the hereditary principle. The King strived to keep out of the battle, believing that a wholesale creation of peers would in effect destroy the House of Lords, and that by agreeing to such action he would inevitably bring the Crown into the political crisis. In the end he told the Prime Minister in confidence that he would only agree to create the necessary number of peers after a second general election had been held on the issue of the Parliament Bill. On Friday, May 6, 1910, following an attack of bronchitis, the King suffered a series of heart attacks, and died. In the upsurge of national grief that followed his death there was a truce in the constitutional controversy, but a conference set up to try to resolve the issue broke down in November. King George V, in granting a dissolution to Asquith, also gave him a secret guarantee that he would create the required number of peers if it proved necessary. In the general election of December, 1910, the results were very similar to those of January, and early in the

The Liberal Government's Parliament Bill for reforming the House of Lords came before the House of Commons in July, 1911, when Mr Asquith stood at the table for some forty minutes without being able to make himself heard above a barrage of hostile shouting. The Speaker was forced to adjourn the House after the Prime Minister had warned that the Government would be compelled to invoke the prerogative of the Crown if the Lords did not restore the Bill to its original form.

The summer of 1911 was one of almost continuous industrial crisis, with railwaymen, firemen, dockers, miners and other workers involved in disputes, some of them violent, in many parts of the country. Here policemen with

drawn truncheons escort a wagon of food supplies across Tower Bridge against attempts by striking dockers to prevent its movement.

following year, after the King's agreement to the creation of peers had been made public, the House of Lords gave way and the Parliament Bill was passed.

The violent turn of British politics that had so concerned King Edward before his death over the issues of the 'People's Budget' and Parliamentary reform was even more evident over the Irish Question, which was to continue to plague this country during the years between the death of Edward and the outbreak of the First World War. It was an issue that not only split the English political parties, but caused divisions within them. The failure of Gladstone's attempts to introduce Home Rule for Ireland by constitutional means had led, at the turn of the century, to the formation of a variety of extreme Irish nationalist movements demanding an independent Republic, and gradually to the development of a Protestant reaction in Ulster and to the idea of partition. In 1912 the Government introduced a Home Rule Bill that proposed a separate Parliament for Ireland and suggested the possibility of separate Parliaments for England, Scotland and Wales along federal lines, with an Imperial Parliament remaining at the head in London. The obvious omission in the Bill was any provision for the Ulster minority, and it was on this failure that the parties at Westminster took their stands. The Conservative and Unionist Party, now led by Bonar Law, was determined to defeat the Bill, and ready to aggravate the situation in Ulster in order to do so. Bonar Law encouraged the Ulstermen, led by Sir Edward Carson, to prepare to resist by force if necessary. The Liberals, on the other hand, who were dependent at Westminster on the support of the Irish Nationalist Party, led by John Redmond, could not compromise on the Bill and could do nothing effective to prevent the armed build-up by extremists of the Irish Volunteers, a force designed to counter Carson's Ulster Volunteers. In March, 1914, the Curragh Mutiny took place, when 58 army officers stationed in Ireland, and forming a part of an English Army unit expected to have to carry out the 'coercion' of Ulster, resigned. Ireland was rapidly drifting into civil war when it became engulfed in the greater conflict in 1914, though the Home Rule Bill was then passed, together with an amendment excluding the six counties, but put on one side for the duration of the war.

The resort to violence became an obstinate characteristic of the four years leading up to the outbreak of the First World War. The summer of 1911 was one of almost continuing industrial crises. There was a

Riots in Liverpool in August, 1911, brought out an armoured motor vehicle and a military escort to accompany prison vans through the streets to Walton Gaol.

national railway strike which, though it lasted only two days, reflected a discontent that was common to many industrial workers. The main cause was the lag in wages, which were failing to keep pace with the rising cost of living. But workers were also angry about the non-recognition of their unions and about the 'Osborne judgment' of the House of Lords, which denied trade unions the right to spend any part of their funds for political purposes. The decision struck at the heart of the new Labour Party, which was created from the Labour Representation Committee in 1906 and which was based on the growing trade union movement, and was ultimately reversed by the passing of the Trade Union Act of 1913, which permitted any union to take political action provided that it first obtained the authority of its members by ballot, and provided that any individual who wished might 'contract out' from a political levy. The rail strike was ended, largely through the conciliatory efforts of Lloyd George, and the settlement led to the passing of the Railway Traffic Act of 1913, which enabled the railway companies to increase their rates in order to meet rising labour costs, and to the amalgamation in the same year of the three railway unions into one National Union of Railwaymen.

The railwaymen were not the only workers determined on direct action to improve their wages and conditions of work. During 1911 sailors, firemen, miners, dockers and others were involved in disputes in many parts of the country, and it seemed that no sooner was one settlement made in one part of the country than another violent dispute flared up somewhere else. Many of the disputes by-passed the trade union representatives and were perhaps the fiercer for being unofficial. There were many street fights, and in Manchester, Liverpool and Wales police reinforcements were called in, together with some Army units. Two men were shot dead in Liverpool, and another two in Llanelly. From February to April, 1912, there was a national miners' strike in support of a demand for a minimum wage. The Government intervened with some reluctance, and agreed to sponsor legislation to set up district boards to fix wages. This was not what the miners were seeking, but it proved enough to end the strike. Later in 1912 the London Lightermen, dockers and carters went on strike, but this ended inconclusively.

The relative failure of such limited strikes (Board of Trade figures showed that not more than 25 per cent of trade disputes in the Edwardian era resulted in settlements favourable to the men) increased the pressure for larger unions organised over a whole industry, and thus more capable of exerting effective influence on the employers. Only the railwaymen

Two men were shot dead by troops after the Riot Act had been read following the destruction of railway carriages, trucks and other equipment by a rioting mob at Llanelly in August, 1911.

achieved this before the war, but out of the same pressure came, in 1913, the idea of the 'Triple Alliance', composed of miners, transport workers and railwaymen, which could bring the country to a standstill at any time by calling a general strike.

Some of those who took part in or campaigned for direct action were undoubtedly motivated by syndicalist ideas adopted from France, though the influence of syndicalism was not as great as was thought at the time. In 1912 a pamphlet issued by a group of Welsh miners, and called *The Miner's Next Step,* was given a good deal of attention. It advocated drastic and militant action, including 'irritation' strikes and go-slows with the aim of reducing profits and thus preparing the way for the elimination of capitalism and its replacement by a Central Production Board which would, armed with a statistical department to ascertain the needs of the people, 'issue its demands on the different departments of industry, leaving to the men themselves to determine under what conditions and how the work should be done'. This, the pamphlet concluded, 'would mean real democracy in real life'. The publication of these ideas caused great concern and led many who might have been more sympathetic

to the grievances of workers to fear that the wave of strikes in these years represented not just an attempt to improve wages and conditions of work but the beginning of a revolution.

Though some Edwardian political thinkers strived to develop syndicalist ideas, or to adapt them to the English situation, the influence of syndicalists on Edwardian England proved to be slight. The main influence behind the wave of strikes was the fall in real wages resulting from price increases, a situation that the Edwardian worker was better able to comprehend and respond to than his predecessors. He was also more ready to be critical of the failure of Parliament to remedy the situation, and far more aware of what life ought to be like. Workers were no longer content that their lives 'should remain mere alternations between the bed and the factory,' as Winston Churchill suggested. 'They demand time to look about them, time to see their homes by daylight, to see their children, time to think and read and cultivate their gardens — time, in short, to live.'

More sensational in its impact on the times was the violence and unrest caused by the campaign for women's suffrage. The increasing activism of this campaign was organised by the Women's Social and Political Union, which had been founded by Mrs Emmeline Pankhurst and her daughter Christabel in 1903. Its militancy was largely triggered by the disappointment experienced by its supporters at the

Top, fighting broke out between rival crowds of Catholic and Protestant demonstrators on the Celtic Park Football Ground in Belfast on September 14, 1912. More than 100 people were hurt.

Bottom, the car carrying Mr and Mrs Winston Churchill to a meeting at Belfast in February 1912 was held up by angry crowds protesting at the Government's Home Rule Bill.

particularly after the Liberal Government, many of whose members had expressed support for their cause, came to power in 1906. The members of the WSPU, or suffragettes as they came to be called (as opposed to suffragists, who were the members of the milder movements known as the National Union of Women's Suffrage Societies), resorted to a programme of harassment of Ministers, planting bombs in their houses and besieging the House of Commons. When they were arrested they chose prison rather than the payment of fines, and when in prison often went on hunger strike, when they were subjected to the miseries of forced feeding. The campaign became even more militant after the failure of a Conciliation Bill brought in by the Government in 1910. The immediate result was the notorious 'Black Friday' in November of that year, when women demonstrating in Parliament Square were roughly treated by the police. But the lack of judgment shown by Mrs Pankhurst and her supporters, and the indiscriminacy of their targets, undoubtedly aggravated many of those influential Ministers, such as Winston Churchill and Lloyd George, who would otherwise have been responsive to their cause. The result was that arguments against

Above left, King George V presented the young Prince of Wales to the Welsh people after his investiture in Caernarvon in 1911.

Above right, some fifty women, most of them domestic servants, called on the Chancellor of the Exchequer, David Lloyd George, at the Treasury to protest about the National Insurance Bill.

giving women the vote were given greater consideration than they deserved.

One of those who presented such arguments was Sir Almroth E. Wright, a distinguished bacteriologist who wrote a long letter to *The Times* in March, 1912, in which he argued that militant suffragettes were sexually and intellectually embittered, comprising the excess female population (there were about 1,200,000 more females than males in Britain at this time) who would have done better to have gone abroad to find their mates. He argued that government required physical force, intellectual stability and an appreciation of standards of abstract morality; women were in his opinion deficient in all three qualities. That such straightforward prejudice should have been treated seriously and with great respect in the press and the

A new form of social entertainment, known as a "jolly" and designed to do away with "the staid conventionality of an ordinary party", was introduced into London society in 1911.

King George opened the great Chingford Reservoir, which had an area larger than Hyde Park, on March 15, 1913.

The new Cunard liner *Aquitania*, 902 feet long and able to carry more than 4,000 passengers and crew, shortly before its launching on the Clyde in 1913.

The most dramatic and most public gesture of the Suffragette campaign occurred on June 4, 1913, when Emily Wilding Davison threw herself in front of the horses as they rounded Tattenham Corner in the Derby. She brought

down the King's horse, *Anmer*, and injured herself so severely that she died in hospital a few days later.

The campaign for women's suffrage was waged in increasingly violent form throughout the decade before the First World War. In 1908 *The Illustrated London News* published, above, the drawing by H.H. Flere which posed the question "Which is fitter to have a vote?" In the same year women chained themselves to the grille of the Ladies' Gallery in the House of Commons, above right, while others, suffragists rather than suffragettes, marched through the streets of London to press for their right to vote. When some women were imprisoned for their violent acts they went on hunger strike, and were subjected to forcible feeding, opposite page.

House of Commons showed to what extent the suffragettes had damaged their cause, though Sir Almroth's letter was effectively answered in *The Times* by Mrs Winston Churchill:

'After reading Sir Almroth Wright's able and weighty exposition of women as he knows them the question seems no longer to be "Should women have votes?" but "Ought women not to be abolished altogether?" . . . We learn from him that in their youth they are unbalanced, that from time to time they suffer from unreasonableness and hypersensitiveness, and that their presence is distracting and irritating to men in their daily lives and pursuits. If they take up a profession, the indelicacy of their minds makes them undesirable partners for their male colleagues. Later on

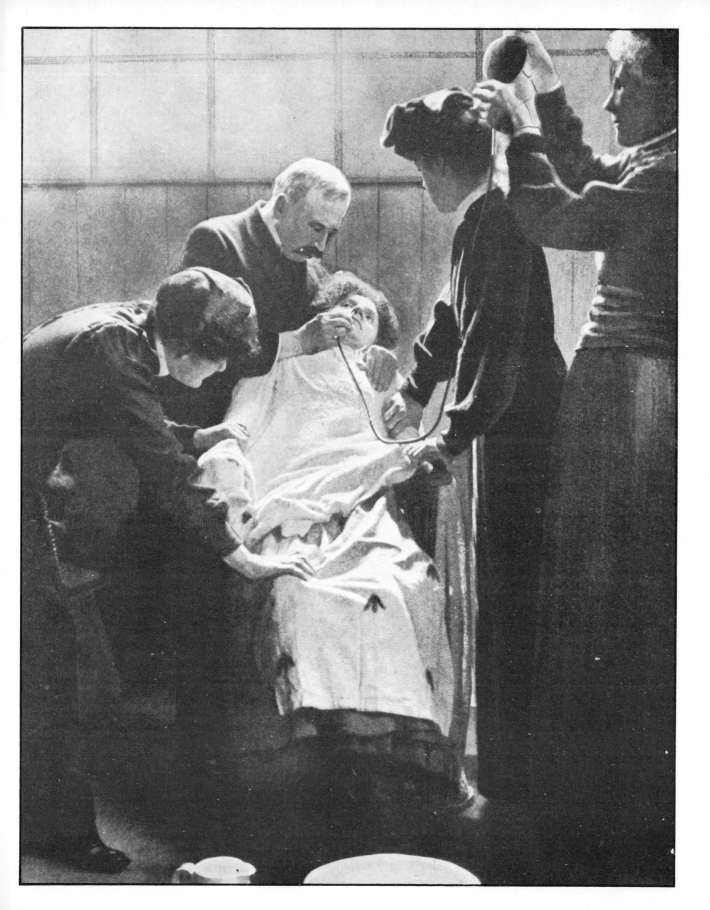

in life they are subject to grave and long-continued mental disorders, and if not quite insane, many of them have to be shut up . . . Cannot science give us some assurance, or at least some ground of hope, that we are on the eve of the greatest discovery of all — ie, how to maintain a race of males by purely scientific means?'

One of the most militant of the suffragettes was Emily Wilding Davison, the holder of a first-class honours degree at Oxford, who had been in prison on a number of occasions for setting fire to letter boxes and other crimes carried out in the name of women's suffrage. On June 4, 1913, she was at Epsom, where she threw herself in front of the horses as they rounded Tattenham Corner to enter the straight for the finish of the Derby. She brought down the King's horse and injured herself so severely that she died in hospital a few days later. It was the most dramatic and the most public gesture of the suffragette campaign, but though the movement organised a great funeral procession through London for her, which was watched by a large and mainly silent crowd, it changed nothing. Neither did the final acts of vandalism carried out by the suffragettes in 1914, which included setting fire to many public buildings, planting bombs in Westminster Abbey, smashing exhibits in the British Museum and damaging paintings in the National Gallery and the Royal Academy. This was the last fiery outburst of suffragette activity, which ended when war broke out in August. The campaign achieved the publicity it sought, but never gained the general sympathy it also badly needed, and which was rapidly and most effectively won by the conduct of women during the war.

Like the conflict over Irish Home Rule and that between the 'bosses' and the 'workers', the suffragette dispute had been carried on with a violence and in an atmosphere of crisis that became all too familiar in the last few years of what is called the Edwardian era, though these events in fact took place during the years after the King had died. But these years are rightly classified as Edwardian because the events had a natural continuity with the earlier years of the twentieth century, and because 1914 brought a convulsion far greater than the death of the King in 1910, and a more conclusive end to an era. These last four years were notable also for their almost total preoccupation with events at home. For though the British people were well enough informed about events abroad, and even vaguely thought there might be a war in Europe some day (and were cautious enough to ensure that at least the Navy was ready for it), neither the British public nor the British Government expected war to break out in 1914. Even in July

"If you would have peace, prepare for war." So ran the caption to the page, above, published in *The Illustrated London News* in 1908, showing the price the major nations of the world were then paying for their naval forces. The Navy indeed had not stopped preparing for war, and spent the early years of the century developing submarines (No 3 is seen in dry dock at Portsmouth in 1902), torpedo boats (views at Tower Bridge in 1908, above right), and giant battleships such as the *Iron Duke,* right, which was completed in 1914 to become flagship of the Home Fleet.

the Cabinet, which met that month for a rare discussion of foreign affairs, believed that, though war seemed likely between the four Continental powers following the Sarajevo assassination, Britain would not be involved. Mr Harold Macmillan, who was an undergraduate at Oxford in the summer of 1914, has described in *Winds of Change* (1966) the impact of the declaration of war:

'The First War, in contrast to the Second, burst like a bombshell upon ordinary people. It came suddenly and unexpectedly — a real "bolt from the blue". It is true that the large expansion of the German Navy was regarded by many informed observers as a serious portent. But the German retreat at Agadir and the

The British Fleet assembled in July, 1914, for a naval review at Spithead, where this photograph of a line of dreadnoughts was taken. The Navy was thus manned and ready for action when war was declared in the following month.

A more penetrative torpedo was designed to overcome the heavier armour-plating with which newer warships were equipped.

A steam-powered caterpillar tractor designed for hauling big guns over heavy ground.

The King on board HMS *Iron Duke* at Spithead.

Top, a machine-gun being tested on board a French aircraft as a new means of aerial warfare.

Bottom, hauling guns by motor instead of horses.

155

somewhat better relations that followed seemed reassuring. Indeed, in the summer of 1914 there was far more anxiety about a civil war in Ireland than about a world war in Europe. Certainly, had we been told, when we were enjoying the carefree life of Oxford in the summer term of 1914, that in a few weeks all our little band of friends would abandon for ever academic life and rush to take up arms, still more, that only a few were destined to survive a four years' conflict, we should have thought such prophecies the ravings of a maniac.'

It was not only on ordinary people that the approach of war fell like a bombshell. Government Ministers were divided until almost the moment of the declaration about the need to go to war, and so was the press. *The Times* had argued at the end of July that Britain's intervention might be necessary to preserve the balance of power. Many other papers took the opposite view. British honour was not involved, declared the *Manchester Guardian*, and there was not a shred of a reason 'for thinking that the triumph of Germany in a European war in which we had been neutral would injure a single British interest, however small, whereas the triumph of Russia would create a situation for us really formidable.' Probably half the members of the Liberal Government shared this view, and believed that Britain could and should keep out of the war unless directly attacked, and no doubt their view was representative of a large body of opinion in the country. But opinion changed rapidly on August 2, when Germany declared war on France and demanded the right to move through Belgium in order to launch its attack. Belgium refused and appealed to Britain as a guarantor of Belgian neutrality. On August 3 the Foreign Secretary, Sir Edward Grey, explained the situation to the House of Commons and secured the agreement of all but a few MPs to the delivery of an ultimatum to Germany demanding the withdrawal of its troops by midnight of August 4. No reply was received and so, to the surprise of most Britons and to the amazement of the German Chancellor, who could not believe that Britain would fight for what he described as 'a scrap of paper', began what *The Illustrated London News* was immediately to call 'The Great War of 1914'.

On August 3, 1914, the Foreign Secretary, Sir Edward Grey, informed the House of Commons of the delivery of an ultimatum demanding the withdrawal of German troops from Belgium by midnight of the following day. It was when this ultimatum had been ignored that Grey, looking out of his window in the Foreign Office, commented: "The lamps are going out all over Europe; we shall not see them lit again in our lifetime."

SELECTED BIBLIOGRAPHY

Julian Amery: The Life of Joseph Chamberlain (Macmillan, 1951)

Asa Briggs (editor): They Saw It Happen, 1897-1940 (Basil Blackwell, 1960)

Gordon Brook-Shepherd: Uncle of Europe (Collins, 1975)

Robert Cecil: Life in Edwardian England (Batsford, 1969)

Randolph Churchill: Winston S. Churchill, Vol 2 1901-1914 (Heinemann, 1967)

Virginia Cowles: Edward VII and his Circle (Hamish Hamilton, 1956)

Maud F. Davies: Life in an English Village (Allen & Unwin, 1909)

Alan Delgado: The Annual Outing and Other Excursions (George Allen & Unwin, 1977)

Sir Robert Ensor: England 1870-1914 (Oxford University Press, 1936)

D. F. Fleming: The Origins and Legacies of World War I (Allen & Unwin, 1968)

R. H. Gretton: Modern History of the English People, (1880-1922) (Secker & Warburg, 1930)

F. J. C. Hearnshaw (editor): Edwardian England (Benn, 1933)

Christopher Hibbert: Edward VII (Allen Lane, 1976)

Alan Jackson: Semi-detached London (Allen & Unwin, 1973)

Sir Sidney Lee: King Edward VII (Two volumes, 1925 and 1927)

Jack London: People of the Abyss (Isbister, 1903)

Harold Macmillan: Winds of Change (Macmillan, 1966)

Philip Magnus: King Edward VII (John Murray, 1964)

C. F. G. Masterman: The Condition of England (Methuen, 1910)

André Maurois: King Edward and his times (Cassell, 1933)

Keith Middlemas: The Life and Times of Edward VII (Weidenfeld and Nicolson, 1972)

Harold Nicolson: Small Talk (Constable, 1937)

Simon Nowell-Smith (editor): Edwardian England (Oxford University Press, 1964)

Ronald Pearsall: Edwardian Life & Leisure (David & Charles, 1973)

Henry Pelling: Modern Britain 1885-1955 (Nelson, 1960)

Sir Charles Petrie: Scenes of Edwardian Life (Eyre & Spottiswoode, 1965)

Sir Frederick Ponsonby: Recollections of Three Reigns (Eyre & Spottiswoode, 1951)

W. MacQueen Pope: Give Me Yesterday (Hutchinson, 1957)

J. B. Priestley: The Edwardians (Heinemann, 1970)

Donald Read: Edwardian England (Harrap, 1972); Documents from Edwardian England (Harrap, 1973)

B. Seebohm Rowntree: Poverty, A Study of Town Life (1901)

Victoria Sackville-West: The Edwardians (The Hogarth Press, 1930)

D. C. Somervell: Modern Britain (Methuen, 1941)

David Thomson: England in the 19th Century, 1815-1914 (Penguin, 1950)

Flora Thompson: Lark Rise to Candleford (Oxford University Press, 1945)

J. C. Trewin: The Edwardian Theatre (Basil Blackwell, 1976)

INDEX